The Four Levels of Happiness

Robert Spitzer, S.J., Ph.D.

The Four Levels of Happiness

Your Path to Personal Flourishing

SOPHIA INSTITUTE PRESS
Manchester, New Hampshire

Sophia Institute Press
Box 5284, Manchester, NH 03108
1-800-888-9344
www.SophiaInstitute.com

Sophia Institute Press is a registered trademark of Sophia Institute.

hardcover ISBN 979-8-88911-234-1

ebook ISBN 979-8-88911-235-8

Library of Congress Control Number: 2024932578

First printing

Contents

The Four Levels of Happiness

1

⚜

Why Am I Not Happy?

Why am I not happy?

If you're asking that question, you're not alone. In fact, you're in the large majority.

A Harris poll in 2017[1] found that less than a third—33 percent—of Americans felt that they were happy. The highest number the annual poll had ever measured was 35 percent. And all this was before the COVID-19 pandemic, which sent happiness ratings plummeting.

Unhappiness is the norm in our world. Most people are unhappy. Yet we know in our hearts that unhappiness is *not normal*. It comes as a *surprise* to us that we're not happy.

More than twenty-three hundred years ago, the ancient Greek philosopher Aristotle taught that happiness is the ultimate goal of all human existence. Other things we want are subordinate: we want them so that we will be happy. Why do we want money? To be happy. Why do we want love? To be happy. But we want happiness for its own sake. You can't ask, "*Why* do we want to be happy?" We just do. We want it because it is our nature.

---

[1] Alexandra Sifferlin, "Here's How Happy Americans Are Right Now," *Time*, July 26, 2017, https://time.com/collection/guide-to-happiness/4871720/how-happy-are-americans/.

The Four Levels of Happiness

So why are we unhappy if we're made for happiness? What's keeping us from being happy?

I'm going to try to answer that question for you, and I'm going to try to show you how you can work toward happiness. But the first thing I'm going to have to do is show you what *isn't* the answer, because you'll find a lot of people trying to sell you wrong answers.

✳

Some of us turn to pleasure for happiness. And marketers definitely encourage us to do so because they can sell us momentary pleasures.

There are lots of things that bring us pleasure. Good food is one example. Maybe you really like fresh strawberries. And look! They're on sale right now! You could get a pound of fresh strawberries, and you could eat strawberries with whipped cream, and that would make you happy, wouldn't it?

Unfortunately, the answer is no. You would enjoy the strawberries, that's true, but they wouldn't make you happy. If you were an unhappy person before you ate the strawberries and whipped cream, then afterward you'd be an unhappy person full of strawberries and whipped cream. They tasted good while you were eating them, but they didn't make a permanent change in your life. And you can't just keep eating strawberries and whipped cream forever. Every pleasure is like that: you reach a point very quickly where the pleasure turns to misery.

That's true even of completely innocent pleasures, like fresh strawberries. They're good for you, at least in moderation. But you can eat too many of them, and then you're going to suffer the consequences. And there are other pleasures that lead to much more than a bellyache.

Those miseries that come from too much pleasure feel all the worse because we know that we have no one to blame but ourselves. Our conscience hurts as much as our stomach when we eat too many strawberries: "Why wasn't I more careful? Even a five-year-old knows that eating too much of a good thing is a bad idea. Why was I dumber than a five-year-old?"

So pleasure isn't enough to make us happy. In fact, pleasure can make us miserable. Of course, that doesn't mean that pleasure is a bad thing: it just means that it isn't the route to lasting happiness.

But then what is?

~~~

Some of us look for happiness in success. It's not always easy to define what "success" is, but we usually mean having more of something than other people have—more money, or a higher position, or a bigger house, or a better car.

But why do we want those things?

Well, that's hard to say. If your car starts when you turn the key, if it's comfortable to sit in while you drive, if it gets you where you're going on time, then why should you care if your neighbor has a car that costs twice as much?

But we do care. We constantly measure ourselves against other people. We divide the world into winners and losers. The one who drives the nicest car wins.

Human beings are naturally competitive, and there's a good reason for everything that's natural. Just like the reward and punishment of pleasure and pain, competition drives us to get things done that need to be done. It pushes us harder than mere pleasure and pain can, and it makes us think of the future when pleasure and pain keep us stuck in the present.

But, just like pleasure, competitiveness doesn't lead to any lasting happiness. People who look to competition for their happiness usually end up miserable. They may reach the peak of success, but they always feel as if their positions are threatened. Think of all the tyrants and dictators in history: How many of them were known for their lives of quiet peace and contentment? Not many. In fact, I can't think of a single one. They all spent their whole careers worrying about what might happen if this or that went wrong: "What if my opponents turn the people against me? What if there's a secret conspiracy to assassinate me? What if my cook is poisoning my food right now?"

So ambition isn't what we're looking for. It's a good thing in its place, but it isn't the route to lasting happiness.

Some of us turn to politics for happiness. After all, don't we want to fix what's wrong with the world? And isn't that what every politician promises to do? Isn't that what we promise *ourselves* when we start getting into politics? If we could just get *this* law passed, or *this* program implemented, or *this* expensive piece of infrastructure built, then we'd be on our way to fixing what's wrong with the world. Or if we could just get *this* candidate elected—she's so wise and virtuous that she'd certainly make all the right choices.

And if we fixed what was wrong with the world, we'd all be happy. Wouldn't we?

But politics is not a good bet for happiness. In fact, there's good evidence that people are less happy the more they think about politics. Eventually, the ultimate expression of politics is civil war, where we decide that standing up for some principle we hold or righting some injustice we perceive is so important to our happiness that you must either agree with us or die. People who live in countries torn by civil war are not happy. You're probably willing to take my word for that, but the statistics back me up too. The countries that score lowest on happiness surveys are the ones where civil wars have been going on for a long time.

So it looks as though politics won't bring us happiness either. I should point out again that I don't mean we shouldn't care about politics. We should do all we can to make sure our country is well governed. It's our duty as citizens and neighbors.

But politics won't make us happy by itself. We won't find a political solution to the happiness problem.

Then where will we find it?

Some people turn to love for happiness, and they're on the right track. Isn't love all you need? Won't love make us happy?

It certainly is true that human love is a good thing.

But if you want proof that human love isn't all it takes to make us happy, all you have to do is tune in to your local country music station for fifteen minutes. There's a reason so many sad songs show up in the playlist—just like there's a reason so many murders are described as "crimes of passion." Love is a strong feeling, and it doesn't always lead us to happiness. It can bring out the worst and most selfish parts of our nature.

Still, love is pushing us in the right direction. It makes us think of someone other than ourselves, and in more than a competitive way. For the first time, we're thinking about how *we* could make someone *else* happy.

We're built for that. Empathy is also part of the equipment that comes with being human. We have a capacity for feeling what others feel, so what others feel has an effect on our own happiness.

And it certainly is true that forming human relationships is a big part of happiness.

The longest of all long-term psychological studies is a Harvard cohort study that has been going on for more than eighty years.[2] Its observations aren't all that surprising, but it's useful to know that science confirms what everybody already knew. Money can't buy happiness. Success can't buy it either. Close human relationships are better predictors of long-term happiness than anything material or any measure of worldly success.

So you're definitely on the right track if you're thinking of love as the road to happiness. You're doing far better than if you stopped at pleasure or success.

But there's even more to life than love.

Some of the happiest people you'll ever meet are people who have nothing. At least they have nothing material. What they *do* have is a strong spiritual life.

Research bears this out too. "Study after study has found that religious people tend to be less depressed and less anxious than nonbelievers, better able to handle the vicissitudes of life than nonbelievers." A study in Europe found that belonging to a religious organization was the only social activity that was a predictor of long-term happiness. Even charity work, divorced from religion, didn't have that effect.[3] A Pew Research Center study found a

---

[2] Liz Mineo, "Good Genes Are Nice, but Joy Is Better," *Harvard Gazette*, April 11, 2017, https://news.harvard.edu/gazette/story/2017/04/over-nearly-80-years-harvard-study-has-been-showing-how-to-live-a-healthy-and-happy-life/.

[3] Bryan Walsh, "Does Spirituality Make You Happy?," *Time*, August 7, 2017, https://time.com/4856978/spirituality-religion-happiness/.

"striking" gap in happiness between actively religious people and religiously unaffiliated individuals in the United States.[4] Over and over, studies come to the same conclusion—and they're not studies done by religious organizations.

We have to recognize, then, that the spiritual life is part of human nature too. We're built to seek pleasure and avoid pain. We're built to be competitive. We're built to feel empathy with other people. And we're built to look for a higher truth beyond what we can see and feel.

I think what this means is that we're designed to climb up a four-rung ladder of happiness. To put it a different way, we have four main kinds of desires, and they're all important—but they're arranged in an ascending scale. If we want to be *happy*, we have to take them all into account.

That's what I want to help you do. I want to help you find your own happiness by showing you where to look for it.

Let me emphasize that this isn't a book that's only for Catholics, or even only for Christians. Just by seeing my name on the cover, you already know that I have opinions about religion. You know where I stand, and I do think you'd be better off if you stood there with me. But you don't have to agree with my religious beliefs to get something out of this book. I think a Buddhist or a Muslim or a Presbyterian will find it very helpful. You do have to accept that there's a spiritual dimension to life, though, because I'm convinced—and the science backs me up on this—that you won't reach lasting happiness without taking the spiritual into account.

---

4   Joey Marshall, "Are Religious People Happier, Healthier? Our New Global Study Explores This Question," Pew Research Center, January 31, 2019, https://www.pewresearch.org/fact-tank/2019 /01/31/are-religious-people-happier-healthier-our-new-global-study -explores-this-question/.

The Four Levels of Happiness

This book isn't going to be an easy little magic happiness pill. Think of all the money that people spend on weight loss. If you come across a book that promises one easy secret that will get rid of excess weight and keep it off without any effort, you know it's a lie. There's no one-step secret. There are different ways to reach the goal, but they're all going to take work. What you *can* do is know what the evidence says about what *will* work and use that as a guide to how you should apply your efforts.

Happiness is the same way. There's no royal road to happiness. You're going to have to do the work. But what this book can do for you is show you what the evidence says about what really will lead you to happiness—and, just as important, what's likely to lead you off the road into the swamp. Happiness doesn't mean no bad things will ever happen to you again. It does mean, though, that you can enjoy the good things and weather the bad things. In our life on earth, that's the best anyone can hope for—and it's a very good life to live.

So, if you're ready, we'll start our quest at the beginning. What *is* happiness? That's the first question we have to answer.

2

⨹

What Is Happiness?

Happiness is the fulfillment of desire.

So if we want an ice-cream cone, and we get an ice-cream cone, we're happy, right?

No. If that were all there was to it, then you wouldn't be reading this book. You'd just be eating ice cream.

Because we're complex intelligent beings, we always have multiple desires on multiple levels. So you can want an ice-cream cone and *get what you want* and still be unhappy. Why is that? Because that ice-cream cone wasn't the only thing you wanted. At the same time, you might want to be promoted to branch manager and to have the empty storefronts in your neighborhood filled in. These are also desires, and you have a lot more besides those. I'd guess that you could name a dozen desires off the top of your head that you have right now. A can of soda, a trip to Paris, a raise, a new car, a change in politics, peace on earth—it doesn't take much effort to fill a page with things you want. And you can't usually have them all at once.

We humans have this problem because we have a greater capacity than any other creature. We've traded simplicity for ability.

Some creatures do very well with simplicity. Sponges, for example, live a life that gets simpler when they grow up. They start out as moving creatures with a tiny and primitive brain to control their movements. Along with that control comes a primitive set of responses to the environment — pleasure and pain — to guide the creatures toward what they need and away from what will kill them. Then the sponges find a place to attach themselves, and they don't need to do all that heavy thinking anymore. So they eat their own brains. The useless brain is digested into the body, and the sponge is left with almost no desires.

That simplicity is perfectly suited for a life of sitting on a rock and digesting whatever happens to pass through in the seawater. But for a more complex lifestyle it doesn't work.

Animals that move around need more brain power, which means they need more desires. They need to have pleasure and pain to motivate them to seek what they need for their own well-being and for the reproduction of the species, and to avoid what will harm them. This means that they're likely to have more than one desire going on at a time, and there has to be some mechanism in the brain to prioritize the desires. You can watch that going on by putting out a treat for a squirrel right by your foot. The squirrel really wants the treat, but the squirrel is very reasonably afraid of the big creature — you — standing right beside the treat. The desire for something tasty conflicts with the desire not to be harmed by a big scary human, and the squirrel may spend quite a long time shuffling back and forth, tail flapping, getting closer and then retreating, before it finally reaches out for the treat or finally gives up and goes away to find a treat in a less hazardous position.

Now we see why happiness gets to be more than ice-cream cones and warm puppies so quickly.

So, although the principles of pleasure and pain lead us toward what we need and away from what will kill us, they aren't perfect.

What Is Happiness?

But it's worth stopping for a while to think about their purpose, because we need to understand both why they're *part* of our happiness and also why they can never be the whole thing.

Trying to Define Happiness

Everybody wants to be happy—we all agree about that. But as soon as we start asking what happiness is, we stop agreeing.

Is happiness a feeling? Is it a state of being? Is it temporary or permanent? Can we be "happy" even when we're sad? Can we decide to be happy, or does happiness depend on circumstances beyond our control?

Instead of defining happiness, most of us probably just give up and start naming examples of things we like. Happiness is a warm puppy. Happiness is a big hot fudge sundae with mounds of whipped cream. Happiness is finding a quarter on the sidewalk.

These are all good feelings, but they're not what we mean when we say we want to *be happy*. We don't want to spend our entire lives eating hot fudge sundaes: it would take only a few minutes for our pleasure to turn into misery. On the other hand, we don't want to stop being happy when we stop eating the hot fudge sundae. So it seems that these temporary pleasures aren't what we really mean by happiness when we say that we want to be happy.

Yet many of us never get beyond that definition. If we look at the Wikipedia article on "Happiness," we're likely to get a good idea of how English-speaking people define the term. Wikipedia is always changing, but the overall tone of the article is likely to be the same if you check it out right now. It's a very long article, and it quotes German philosophers, contemporary psychologists, Church Fathers, Sufi mystics, Confucian teachers, and all kinds of thinkers who have tried to tell us what happiness is. But the illustrations are all people smiling and enjoying temporary

13

pleasures—a woman kissing a baby, a class of U.S. Naval Academy graduates tossing their caps in the air.[5] We think of these as pictures of people *being happy*. But the midshipmen's caps don't stay in the air very long. Are those young officers still happy when gravity does its work?

We've all witnessed instances when people have been miserable at the very moment they were having an experience that most of us would think of as pleasant. In fact, we've all been through it ourselves. You can be very sad while eating a hot fudge sundae. You can look out on a field of flowers waving in the breeze on a sunny spring day and feel nothing but gloom.

For the worst examples, we can look at the rich and famous. How many Hollywood actors have killed themselves at the height of their success? How many are in treatment for depression right now? These are the people who practically define success for us. They have money. They have the admiration of millions of people. They can buy whatever they want whenever they want it. If they want twenty-four-hour hot-fudge-sundae service, nothing stops them. But they're miserable. Not all of them, of course—and that's the mystery. Two people live in the same circumstances, with the same opportunities for pleasure, with the same difficulties to overcome, with the same hot fudge sundaes to eat, and one of them is cheerful and the other is morose and suicidal. What's going on?

It gets even harder to figure out when you remember the people who don't have material things and are still happy. There are a lot of those. Think of the poor nun who gives up everything to tend to the sick and dying who have no one else to help them.

[5] "Happiness," Wikipedia, accessed May 27, 2023, https://en .wikipedia.org/wiki/Happiness.

What Is Happiness?

Think of the missionary who gave up the comforts of suburban life to work in the poorest neighborhood in the city. Think of the homeless man who walks down the street singing. Why are these people happy? Not a single one of them has a hot fudge sundae!

So we have two problems to solve. First, why are so many people unhappy when they have everything we think makes people happy? Second, why are so many people happy when they have next to nothing?

It looks as though we need a better definition of happiness than just a series of examples of pleasant things. We begin to see why the ancient philosophers, the Church Fathers, and even most modern psychologists have gone beyond trying to define happiness in terms of a warm puppy.

Still, maybe those pleasant experiences give us a good place to start.

Happiness on Four Levels

Why do we think of pleasant things first when we think of what it means to be happy? It must be because we know that those are things we *desire*, and we think of happiness as the fulfillment of our desires. We're happy if we get what we want. We're unhappy if there's something we really, really want, and we don't have it.

Where we go wrong is in forgetting that there's more than one kind of desire. We see that there are things we want right now, like food or comfort. But as soon as we start to think about it, we realize that there are other things we want, too, things that aren't quite so obvious and material. We want to get ahead in life. We want our children to succeed. We want to love and be loved. We want to be sure of what's going to happen to us when we die.

So it looks as though we're going to have to figure out what we mean when we say, "I want," because it's not always the same thing.

The Four Levels of Happiness

This will help us with our definition of happiness too. We can say now that happiness means the fulfillment of our desires—but we have to take *all* our desires into account.

After studying the problem for years and calling in the help of the best minds that ever existed, I've concluded that there are four kinds of desire, and therefore four kinds of happiness. They arrange themselves in an ascending scale, from the lowest to the highest form of happiness.

First, there's desire for material things—obvious comforts. This kind of desire is built in at the lowest level of our being. Animals have it, too, because it's what keeps them alive. An insect wants to eat and wants not to be eaten. Mice in a laboratory avoid pain and seek pleasure. So we look for food that tastes good because the taste tells us that it will be good to eat. The system isn't perfect: my sense of taste still wants more hot fudge sundae long after prudence tells me I ought to quit. But these deep-seated instincts are the things that keep us alive. They're good things. They're just not all there is.

Second, we have a desire to succeed. It's the kind of desire that comes from *self-consciousness*, which is a strange thing when you think about it. Like all the animals, we're aware of the world around us. But we're also aware that we're aware, which—as far as we can tell—is something only humans do. And we're aware that other people are aware—that they have self-thoughts just as we have self-thoughts. We'll get into this more deeply soon, but the important point for now is that we compare ourselves to other people: "Am I doing better than that one over there? Am I falling behind in my career? What do people think of me as opposed to *her*?" These are questions we can ask only because we know that other people have self-awareness too.

Third, we have a desire for other people to be happy. This is a natural, built-in human trait: the ability to empathize. We'll even give up our own material desires because it makes us happier to see someone else have theirs met. We probably don't do it often enough, but it's a natural human thing to do. And, of course, it works the other way around: if I see someone else unhappy, it can make me unhappy, too, even if I have all the comforts I could possibly want.

Fourth, we have a desire for something beyond this present life. This is going to be controversial—maybe the only controversial desire of the four. But it's necessary to understand that this desire is built in. It's part of our nature. We can deny it or ignore it, but it will be there, and some of our desire is going to be unfulfilled if we don't take it into account.

Knowing that there's more than one kind of desire helps us understand some of the things we were having a hard time understanding before. Why does a famous movie star drown herself in booze, even though she has all the money she could spend and every material comfort she could want? Why does a billionaire jump out of a skyscraper when the stock market goes down and he's reduced to a mere millionaire? Why do we see a poor nun who lives in a tiny room with nothing but seems to be the happiest woman on earth?

The answer to all these questions probably has to do with desires, fulfilled and unfulfilled. Someone who has concentrated on gaining material things and ignored the other three kinds of desire may have a lot of unfulfilled desires gnawing their way to the surface. On the other hand, someone who has learned to place all her hope in things that aren't material may have everything she wants, even if she has just enough material comforts to keep her alive and no more.

The order of those four desires wasn't accidental, as I said. They rise in steps from the most animalistic to the most spiritual. And to reach real happiness, we have to climb that stairway. We can't ignore the lowest step completely—material things are necessary to keep us going. But we can't stop at that step, or at the second, or even at the third. We have to go all the way up to that fourth step, or there will always be something missing, some unfulfilled desire that keeps us from being really happy.

Now you know the whole theme of this book. All the rest of it is going to be an explanation of what you've just read here. We're going to talk about how we know there are different kinds of happiness, and how we know what they are, and how understanding what they are will help us reach the happiness we're looking for. You're not finished with the second chapter, and you already know what the whole book is about.

But it will be worth your while to read the rest. Just hearing me say that there are four kinds of desires isn't convincing. I know I have to work for it if I want to convince you that I'm right. And I think it's important to convince you, because I think your happiness depends on it—and because I have human empathy, my happiness depends on yours.

I also know that of all those four stages of desire the one I'm going to have to work hardest with is the fourth: the transcendent. There's a lot of resistance to the very idea of the transcendent in our culture today. I don't think you can be really happy without acknowledging the transcendent, so I'm going to have to make my case. Before I can convince you that you need to take the spiritual into account to be really happy, I'm going to have to convince you that there is a spiritual realm in the first place. I'm going to have to show you that there's more to life than what we see.

So, let's work our way up the happiness levels, from the lowest kinds of desire to the highest level. We'll start with ice cream—because who doesn't like ice cream?

3

~~~~

Happiness Level 1: Pleasure and Pain and Why We Have Them

Ice cream tastes good. You eat ice cream, and you *may* feel a little jolt of happiness—for a while. Then you want more. So you eat more ice cream, and the cycle repeats. Eventually you've eaten way too much ice cream, and you feel miserable.

What's going on here?

As soon as we're born, we have needs. (In fact, we have needs before we're born, too, but they're taken care of by the automatic functions in our mothers' bodies.) But at any given moment, it's easier to sit and do nothing than it is to get up and do something, even if that something is vital to our continued existence. So, what's going to make us put in that extra effort?

To make sure we survive, both individually and as a species, we have those two fundamental principles that guide our behavior: pleasure and pain. Things that we need to have give us pleasure. Things that we need to avoid give us pain. The system isn't perfect, but it's wonderfully simple. Without even thinking about it, we're motivated to seek out the things that are good for us and avoid the things that are bad for us.

These are impulses we share with the simplest animals, although of course in our case they're developed to a far more sophisticated degree. On the whole, these impulses are very efficient at their jobs. No one has to tell us to avoid things that hurt. We just do, because we hate pain. And no one has to tell us to seek out things that are pleasant to us. We just do, because our brains are built to seek out pleasure.

Pleasure is a drug—literally. There's a chemical in our brains called dopamine that gives us a sense of reward. When we do something pleasant, we get a release of dopamine, and our brains tell us we liked that.

Like many other drugs, though, pleasure can become an addiction. We yearn more and more for that dopamine release, and we need more and more of whatever produced it. That happens because we were built for a much more precarious existence than the one our modern civilization provides for us.

Dopamine, Homeostasis, and the Happiness Balance

Anna Lembke, a psychiatrist who has made studying our addictions her specialty, wrote a book that became a bestseller: *Dopamine Nation*. Her argument is that the things that make our civilization so delightful are the things that are making us depressed. We're miserable because we have so many things to make us happy.

How can that be?

It all goes back to the most basic parts of our brains, the parts we share with animals of all kinds, right down to the reptiles. According to modern research, our misery comes down to the principle of dopamine homeostasis.

I don't expect you to know what those words mean, unless you've heard them on some pop psychologist's YouTube channel. So I'm going to try to explain the basic idea, without getting too deep into technical biological language.

Every living thing has to react to its environment. Plants grow toward the light; they put out roots in the direction of water; they produce different chemicals if pests attack them.

Animals that move need to have more complex reactions to their environments. You remember how sponges begin as mobile creatures, and they have a very simple sort of brain that controls their movements through space. But soon the sponge settles down and attaches itself to a rock, and then the body digests its own brain. Who needs to think when you're spending your life attached to a rock?

Sponges show us that the power of motion is the power of making *decisions*. To make decisions, we have to be able to pick what will be good for us and avoid what will be bad for us. Any animal that fails that simple test won't survive long.

Pleasure and pain, as we said before, are the main motivators to make the right decision. But in human beings there's more to it than just pleasure and pain. That release of dopamine we crave comes with an automatic penalty.

Potato chips taste good. We eat a potato chip, and it puts a little weight on the reward side of our brains.

But our brains are designed to keep that balance—that homeostasis—in the dopamine level. So the brain puts a little weight on the displeasure side to balance out the reward we just got. What will cure that displeasure? Another potato chip!

You can see how this mechanism is very useful in a world where food is scarce. If you lived in a hunter-gatherer society and you found some tasty berries, it would be good to pick and eat a lot of them because you wouldn't know when you were going to find more nutrition like that again. Your body needs that nutrition to keep going.

But we're not living in a hunter-gatherer society. We live in a world where there's always another potato chip. That's the problem with our world of plenty: our brains aren't programmed to deal with it.

You may already have noticed that all this modern research is just telling us what Aristotle told us twenty-three hundred years ago. Moderation in all things—that was his key to happiness. It hasn't changed. Again, it's not enough, but it's a good start.

Everything we do that tips the balance one way or another makes us less happy. But most of us don't have to worry about deliberately tipping the scale toward unhappiness. Our brains are designed to want happiness, as Aristotle told us all those years ago. So the danger is that we'll keep trying to do the things we think will make us happy.

Pleasure Is Not the Same as Happiness

What I've been saying is that we're confusing pleasure with happiness. Pleasure is a momentary thing: it's here and then it's gone, and we need another dose of it to feed our addiction. Happiness is a state of being that can last through quite a bit of pain and unpleasantness.

Aristotle's wisdom is confirmed by modern neurology. We've identified chemicals and processes, but they don't change the observation: Too much pleasure makes us miserable. We become addicts. When we focus on short-term gratification, we spiral further down into the pit of unhappiness we were trying to crawl out of.

On the other hand, if we do something difficult, something that makes us work and do things that are not pleasant in themselves for a reward in the longer term, our brains work to balance out the scale in the other direction. This is why we find hard work rewarding. It's not just the result that we like: the work itself gives us satisfaction because the brain will pile stuff up on the reward side of the scale.

Again, you can see how this is very useful in a more precarious way of life. If your survival depends on building a hut that will keep you out of the weather, then you'd better find the work rewarding. Just avoiding the future pain of death from exposure isn't enough. That's way in the future. Right now, you need to work toward a goal, and you need a strong incentive to keep working.

But you don't have to build a hut for shelter. Once again, our issue is that so many of our most basic problems can be solved instantly. You're hungry? The most work you'll have to do is tearing off a plastic wrapper. You're cold? Change the setting on the thermostat. You need clothes? They never run out of clothes at the shopping mall. Our basic needs are met, and more than met. We don't have to put much effort into it at all.

Even in our jobs, we often don't have to put much effort in to get a paycheck. In fact, the thing people hate most in a job is doing nothing, or at least nothing worthwhile. If you've ever had a job where you just had to sit at work all day with not much to do, you know how excruciatingly dull it was. You couldn't wait for the end of the day to come so you could stop doing nothing at work and go home and do nothing there instead. That's why researchers say that "the single most effective way organizations can achieve a satisfied workforce is to provide their employees with mentally challenging work."[6] That might not have been your first guess, but it fits with everything we've already seen. A job where you work hard and accomplish something is much more satisfying than a job where everything is easy and you don't get anything

---

[6] Timothy A. Judge and Ryan Klinger, "Promote Job Satisfaction through Mental Challenge," in *Handbook of Principles of Organizational Behavior: Indispensable Knowledge for Evidence-Based Management*, ed. Edwin Locke, 2nd ed. (Chichester, UK: John Wiley and Sons, 2009), 119.

done. People who work hard at worthwhile jobs are usually happier. They may even work more hours than they're paid for, just because they want that sense of accomplishment they get when they know the job is done well.

However, there are other reasons for working hard. You've probably been encouraged since early childhood to work hard because it's the way to *get ahead*. You can have a better job, higher pay, and more respect from the people around you if you push your way to the top.

Well, then, will that make you happy?

4

~~~~

Happiness Level 2: Am I as Good as You?

When babies are born, their world is almost completely self-centered. They want food, warmth, comfort—that's about it. They're stuck in that first level of desire, where bodily needs (pleasure and pain) are the beginning and end of their existence.

But children soon learn that there are other people who also have things they want. They learn that the activities other people engage in are fascinating. That's part of our biological programming. Children are built to be sponges, absorbing our language and action and imitating them. That's how we learn. Simple animals have instinct—programmed responses for every situation. But we humans have a long learning period. It gives us adaptability and flexibility no other animal has: instead of a limited set of built-in responses, we can learn from our parents and neighbors how to adapt to the situation in our environment, and then if things change we can figure out how to adapt to the new situation. But the trade-off is a very long period of learning and being helplessly dependent on older people.

Still, it's surprising how fast children learn to recognize that other people have mental lives and needs and desires of their own. And once children learn that, they start to learn how to manipulate those other people.

The Four Levels of Happiness

A World of Other People

This is what the selfish part of us wants from other people. Once we learn that there's an outer world, full of people who are outside of our own mind, we want to control that outer world. We want to make everything in it work for our benefit. Even after we've grown into civilized adults, there's still that selfish part of the brain that wants other people to be things we can manipulate. In the lower parts of our brains, we want every other human being to be our slave. We want to be able to make them do *this*, be *there*, say *that*.

As soon as children start to figure out how to manipulate their parents, the parents have to be very careful. Children will learn that certain behaviors get them what they want. If a tantrum gets them what they want, there will be more and more tantrums. A friend of mine swears he caught his two-year-old rehearsing different styles of crying in front of the mirror. I believe it. Children learn very quickly, and a big part of that learning is finding ways to get what they want out of other people—especially their parents, who are usually the other people they have the most contact with.

This is the beginning of Level 2. We begin to realize that other people have something to do with our happiness. This is already a step up from Level 1, because it takes us out of ourselves and brings us into the outer world of other human beings. Even if we want them all to be perfect servants, at least we understand that there are other human beings, and we begin to consider what they might be thinking and desiring.

Once we get to school, we find a whole world of other human beings. The circle of our world gets a lot larger. We get to know other people our own age. We begin to think about whether we're doing as well as they are.

This kind of thinking seems to be built into human psychology. It's part of what helps us form societies. Are we doing as well as that person over there? Does she have more than we do?

Schools give us every opportunity to compare ourselves to other people. They insist on it. They sort us in grades or forms, so we know right away who has been learning longer. They grade our work, so we know how we're doing in comparison to everybody else. The class is divided into A students, B students, C students, D students, F students—winners and losers and in-betweens. It's not just that we have the chance to compare ourselves to other people in school: it's pretty much required of us.

But even without our grades, there are plenty of ways we can compare ourselves to other people in school. Put a bunch of people the same age together in one place, and they'll start playing the comparison game even without any encouragement:

"Am I more attractive than that person over there?"

"Is that girl smarter than I am? Is that boy faster?"

"Am I shorter than most of the people in my class? Is my skin the wrong color?"

"Do people think I walk funny? Is this shirt too old?"

"Why don't I have as many friends as that boy over there?"

No one has to tell children to compare themselves to other children that way. They just do. It's a natural human instinct. And there are good reasons for it.

Ambition—the Good and the Bad

I call this kind of desire *ego-comparative*. I look at what *you* have and compare it to what *I* have. If I see that you have more—more money, more power, more status—then you're winning and I'm losing. That can make me miserable if I dwell on it, and part of being human is that we *do* dwell on it.

Not that this kind of desire is completely bad. There are good things about it too. Ambition is good to a point. After all, something needs to make us get up and do something with our lives. It's all the more important in a world where our basic needs are met. Why shouldn't I just sit on the couch and scroll through my Facebook feed as long as the food keeps coming? But then I look at you, and you have a better house and a nicer car, and people look up to you. I want that for myself. I'd better get up off the couch.

Ego-comparative desire is the first level of desire that takes us out of ourselves. It can be a strong motivator, and human organizations take advantage of that when they want to get things done.

Think of the military. In an emergency, we need to have soldiers who will obey orders quickly and well, so we train them to be efficient and obedient. It would be easy if we could rely on the patriotic virtue and forward thinking of our soldiers. If they just said to themselves, "I must do this now, so that our country will be defended when it most needs defending, and I will put my best effort into it because I love my country"—well, then, the military would run like clockwork.

But human beings, even good and patriotic ones, don't usually think that way. So we give our soldiers incentives in the form of recognition. Why does a medal motivate a soldier? Why would it make that soldier perform better to know that a small dangling ornament might be added to his uniform? Because the ornament is an implied comparison. It says, "This soldier is *better* than all those soldiers who don't have this medal on their uniforms." It feeds our ego-comparative desire.

Ambition—the desire to be better off than we are—is what motivates us to get to work. In a hunter-gatherer society you would likely eat just as much as you could hunt or gather, so your simple bodily needs and comforts were enough to get you going in the morning. But most of us don't live in hunter-gatherer societies. We live in a culture where we have to plan ahead. Right now, there's food in the refrigerator, and there's gas for the furnace, and there's a couch and endless entertainment streaming on Amazon Prime. Why should I even leave the house? Well, if I want those things to continue, maybe I have to earn some money. But we're not very good at thinking far into the future, or even an hour into the future, and making the decision that will benefit us the most. So we're programmed to compare ourselves to other people. If someone else has more and better things, we want to get out there and equalize the comparison.

This can certainly have good effects. It can, for example, neutralize the powerful appeal of some of those Level 1 desires.

Imagine I'm in school. I want to get ahead. That means I have to get the work done. And that means, even though there's a party Friday night with all the beer I could drink, I have to stay in my room and work because this essay is due by eight o'clock Monday morning. Monday morning is three days away, but I know from experience that I'm going to need all that time to finish the work. If I don't get it done, I'll fail the class. I'll be a failure, and everybody will know I failed. So I do what it takes for my long-term success instead of my short-term fun. And I do it mostly because I want to be a *winner*. I don't want other people to think I'm a failure.

The same point is true when I leave school and go to work. I show up when I'm supposed to show up. I don't leave till quitting time. I may end up putting in overtime once in a while. I practice these habits because I don't want to be left behind. I compare myself to other people, and I see that this is what it takes to be a winner. Since I don't want to be a loser, I put off the pleasures of a comfortable couch and infinite television until all the work is done.

It's a good thing to have some ambition. It makes us live up to our potential, or at least it makes us think a little bit about the future. We need something to take us out of the world of immediate pleasure and pain.

Instead of the simple pleasures of the senses, more abstract things satisfy the second level of desire. We want to be better than other people. We want to look at that person over there and think, "I've done more and better things than he has. People around us respect me more than they respect him. I have more friends. I'm smarter. I have more control over what happens to me. I can tell him what to do, and he has to do it."

Those are the elements that satisfy our lust for comparison. In moderation, they can make us better people than simple sensory pleasure does. They force us to think ahead and plan for the future.

However, the ego-comparative desire can lead to misery very quickly, just as our animal desires can. We have noted the stories of rich Hollywood stars who drowned themselves in alcohol because they thought they weren't good enough, or the ex-billionaire who jumped out of a window because he was reduced to a mere multimillionaire.

But our culture pushes this second level of desire hard. We're constantly prodded to get ahead, to have more money and more stuff. We divide our world into winners and losers, and you'd better be one of the winners.

Marketers love it when we compare ourselves to other people. Our hair is fine—until we see *that* person's hair. What can we do to make our hair as lush and attractive as that? We'll have to buy something that will make our hair better. We have a four-year-old car, and our neighbor's is only a year old. We'll be the laughingstock of the neighborhood! Time for an upgrade. Our shoes are looking a bit old. Everybody's probably staring at our feet, thinking, "Look at those tatty old shoes." We have to keep up appearances if we're going to get ahead. Every time we compare our material possessions to other people's, some marketer sees dollar signs.

But the comparison game can cost us more than money. It can cost us friendships and relationships. It can make us miserable to the point of despair, so we look for a quick solution in alcohol or drugs or other addictions.

This is the secret of the supermodel who destroys her looks with health-ruining addictions, of the multimillionaire who jumps from a skyscraper because he can't face his billionaire friends, of the Hollywood star who drinks himself to death because he thinks he'll never amount to anything. They've all been playing the comparison game. And they've all been losing.

You can always find people better off than you, and you can always find people worse off than you. The problem is that you'll never be the very best. The comparison game is a losing game in the end. You can get a momentary burst of satisfaction from seeing that you have nicer things or a better career than your old friend from high school, but then you meet another old friend from high school, and she's a world-class opera singer or the governor of Maryland, and pretty soon you're back to thinking you're losing the game.

Actually, I find that people tend to fall into three groups. There are people who think they're the winners in life. There are people who think they're the losers in life. And there are a lot of people who fall in between those two groups: sometimes they feel like winners, and sometimes they feel like losers.

All three groups have their problems. Even the winners. I might almost say especially the winners.

The Four Levels of Happiness

The Winners

Isn't it great to be one of life's winners? Well, winning in anything is definitely a good feeling. I'm not going to deny that. But no one wins everything all the time. People who define themselves as winners, though, may feel as though they *have* to win. That sort of self-image can lead to an addiction to ego boosts. You can develop a craving, almost a physical need, for things that make you feel better about yourself. Psychologists call it *narcissism*. It's named for Narcissus, a character in Greek mythology who fell in love with his own reflection. Things didn't end well for him, by the way. In the myth, he was so enchanted with his reflection that he couldn't stop staring at it, until he finally melted away, leaving only the flower that bears his name. Remember, kids: this could happen to you if you're not careful.

Narcissism can lead to compulsive ambition. We already touched on how addiction works when we talked about material pleasures, and this kind of addiction is no different. It actually causes chemical changes in the brain. The ambition becomes a kind of self-medication, as the psychologists call it. You got a big hit from that last ego boost, and you crave that feeling. But it's going to take a *bigger* hit to get the same feeling the next time. What satisfied you before isn't going to satisfy you now. And when the prizes you want are power, superiority, status—well, then, your addiction starts to affect other people. You need to get ahead, and anything that stands in your way has to be eliminated.

Think of any really evil character in history—Nero, Attila the Hun, Robespierre, Hitler, Stalin, Pol Pot—and you'll find someone who was obsessed with being a winner. And probably someone who came to a miserable end too. These were people for whom the last victory was never enough. They needed more power, more authority, more respect—more, more, more—until they literally had nothing left but to conquer the world.

Even if you don't end up with an Alexander the Great complex, though, defining yourself as a winner can make things unpleasant for you, as well as the people around you. You can start to hate the losers. You wish they would just get out of the way. And you start to resent the people who don't respect your winning ways enough: "Why can't they see how much better I am? Why don't they just realize I'm the smartest person in the room?" You start to feel compelled to show other people just how inferior they are. You make them miserable, and your reward is that you're surrounded by miserable people all the time. You hate them for being miserable and making the world around you miserable to be in. You find yourself constantly angry. You may start to find that people don't seem to like you anymore. They think you're arrogant. They don't like to be around you if they know you're always going to think you're better than they are. And that makes you angrier, and people also don't like to be around you if you're going to be angry all the time.

It can be very lonely being a winner.

And you're also constantly worried, especially if you're forced to face some unexpected bad luck. What if we make a mistake and everybody laughs at us? What if we get passed up for the promotion and that kid who just got here last year ends up being our boss? What if the stock market goes down and we're not a millionaire anymore?

Then we might be a *loser!*

But, really, if this is what your life is going to be like, you might be better off thinking of yourself as a loser.

The Losers

Not that it's a picnic feeling like a loser either. I don't have to tell you that, because our twenty-first-century consumer culture will tell you over and over all day. It will also tell you that the activity that will keep you from feeling like a loser is buying something, because the marketing department will never miss the chance to bring your thoughts back to how spending money can make you feel better.

Frankly, feeling like a loser is miserable. You may have spent some time that way yourself. If you have, you know what I'm talking about. Or you may have friends or family who feel as though they're doomed to lose every time in the comparison game, and you've seen what it can do to them.

First of all, when you feel like a loser—when you feel inferior to the people you think of as the winners in life—you're jealous of the winners. Jealousy is never pleasant. There's a reason the medieval theologians put envy in the list of seven deadly sins. It makes you not just a miserable person but also a person who's likely to make other people miserable as well.

You may notice people avoiding you because you make them miserable. "Well, of course," you say. "I'm a loser. What did I expect? Winners have lots of friends. Losers don't. That's what makes us losers."

So you wallow in self-pity, and that makes you more miserable. You may feel very uncomfortable in any situation where you think you might be compared to other people—or any situation outside your comfort zone, which gets smaller and smaller as time goes on. You think that, of course, good things won't happen to you, because good things are for other people. Then, of course, you lose all ambition, which means that good things really won't happen to you, because you take no steps to make them happen.

Some people who feel this way find a way out. "I don't need other people," they say. "I'll go it alone." And it may make you feel better for a while. But the fact is that you do need other people. We're built that way.

In extreme cases, people who put themselves in the "losers" group may begin to wallow in darkness. They may indulge in self-destructive, self-harming behaviors. They may find themselves attracted to the ideas of death and darkness. In severe cases, they kill themselves.

So it's miserable to be a loser. And we already saw that it's miserable to be a winner. Does that mean the best place to be is somewhere in the middle?

Not necessarily.

The In-the-Middles

Most people probably fall somewhere between those who define themselves as winners and those who define themselves as losers. Statistically, then, it's likely that you, the person reading this book, are in the in-between group. If that's true, then I don't have to tell you that it's not always a great place to be. You're reading a book about how to be happy, after all. You know your life isn't perfect.

People who live in that in-between world can face some of the problems of both the winners and the losers. Sometimes you win, and it makes you feel good. But even when you're winning, you know that you might be a loser the next time. That causes anxiety. People in the middle may find themselves constantly worried. You might fall down into the losers' camp at any moment. You're constantly judging how you compare to other people and moving yourself up or down in the rankings depending on what you observe. You may become addicted to the comparison game. You worry that people will stop respecting you, because you constantly judge yourself by how you compare to other people, and you assume other people are judging you the same way. And that ground is constantly shifting as the people around you go up or down momentarily in their struggles. You never know from day to day where you'll stand.

This is a roller-coaster ride, emotionally speaking. In many cases it can lead to what psychologists call impostor syndrome: the feeling that you're only getting by because people don't know how worthless you really are. "You're a fake," your brain tells you. People are bound to find out eventually, and then you'll lose everything.

It's miserable being stuck in the middle when you play the comparison game.

What's the Answer?

What, then, is the answer? If it's bad to be a winner, bad to be a loser, and bad to be somewhere in between, what's left? Doesn't that mean it's bad to be anywhere on the scale?

There's a way out. The cure is to realize that *you are not a thing*.

Think about it: That's what you've been doing to yourself if you've been playing the comparison game. You've been treating yourself like a *thing*—an object whose only value is in how useful it is. A twenty-dollar bill is worth more than a ten-dollar bill. A diamond is worth more than a rhinestone. A lieutenant colonel is worth more than a captain. A driver behind the wheel of a current-year Lexus is worth more than a driver behind the wheel of a ten-year-old Hyundai. You're judging yourself the way you would judge an inanimate object. But you are not inanimate.

You need to realize that you are valuable because you are a human being. You're not valuable because of what you can do or how much money you can bring in.

Fortunately, we humans have a built-in ability to recognize the real value, the infinite value, in other human beings. It's called *empathy*, and it will lead us up the stairs to the next level of desire and fulfillment.

5

~~~~~

Happiness Level 3: Am I Doing Enough for Other People?

We're not just made of hunger and thirst. One of the capabilities built into our nature is empathy, and it's just as important to our happiness as our physical needs.

Empathy comes from a Greek word meaning "in-feeling," and that's exactly what it is. It's our human ability to feel what others feel.

Think about your own experience. When someone you love is happy, you feel happy. When someone you love is sad, you feel sad.

It doesn't even have to be someone you love. You can be walking down the sidewalk, and a random stranger half a block away trips and falls. Immediately you think, "Wow, that hurt!" Your muscles tighten. Your breath catches. Your heart rate changes. It's almost as though the thing that happened to that random stranger happened to you at the same time.

Science confirms what all of us know by experience. If you see someone get hurt, it activates the same parts of your brain that are active when you get hurt yourself. When somebody says, "I feel your pain," it may be just a nice thing to say. But it can also be true in the most literal possible sense. We really do feel another person's pain.

The Four Levels of Happiness

The other person doesn't even have to be real. Think about it: Isn't fiction a strange thing? We read a story, or watch a movie, or see a play, and we care what happens to people who never did exist and never will exist. If we don't care, we don't enjoy the story. Our entertainment works only because we have that built-in capacity for "in-feeling"—for empathy.

There are good reasons for that ability. Our whole society is stronger when we each care what happens to our neighbors. Society starts to break down when we stop caring. If we lose the ability to feel what certain other people are feeling, then those people are simply objects. If they're useful objects, we keep them around as long as we can use them. But more often they're simply in the way. They have the same material needs we have. They want the same things we want. And why should they have the things we want when we could have those things instead?

We don't have to look very far for examples of what happens when we lose empathy with some group of people. History gives us the Holocaust. Today's news gives us something else—a war, a terrorist attack, a mass shooting. At such times, and during such events, we can no longer feel what other people are feeling.

The good news is that empathy is the normal human condition. You feel bad if you read about a mass shooting in the news. Empathy is part of our makeup. We're born with it.

Empathy Is in Our Nature

That's why empathy is an important ingredient in our happiness. It's not as obvious as food or shelter, but it, too, is a basic human function. It shows up very early in our development.

You've seen it happen: a child starts to cry, and then across the room another child starts to cry. There's nothing wrong with that second child, except that something is wrong with the first child. The pain or sadness or whatever it is transmits itself from one mind to another, even if the children are too young to talk.

We go to movies and watch dramas on television. We read novels. We go to plays. Why? These experiences don't feed us, and if they shelter us, it's only incidentally. We have more comfortable shelter at home. Watching the made-up adventures of made-up people doesn't satisfy any of our animal needs. Yet we do need it, as we can see from the way we prioritize it. Americans spend close to ten billion dollars just on going out to the movies every year.[7] We spend almost incalculable amounts on entertainment we consume at home. Walk into an average American living room, and the focus of the whole room is a big-screen TV. And it's not just the TV we spend money on: it's the cable or streaming service that feeds it and the furniture that's specially adapted for sitting on to watch the TV. Everything that happens on that TV is happening to other people, unless you're a TV personality yourself and never watch anything but your own show.

Fiction is an important part of the human experience: we can tell it is just by how much money we spend on it. What this means is that the experiences of other people are important to us. Some part of our happiness depends on the happiness of the people around us — even the fictional people.

Once we understand that, we have our key to the next level of happiness. It's not enough just to have what we want to survive and be comfortable. It's not enough to know that we're doing better than other people. Paradoxically, our happiness depends on how well other people are doing.

---

[7] "Domestic Movie Theatrical Market Summary 1995 to 2023," The Numbers, accessed June 21, 2023, https://www.the-numbers .com/market/.

Scientifically, we can see how this human trait is also important for our survival. Some animals survive by being large and strong. A Bengal tiger hunts alone. Humans are not nearly as strong as Bengal tigers individually, but we form groups to protect ourselves from dangerous predators. The group can overcome the tiger where one solitary human couldn't. But the group doesn't work unless we care about the other people in it. In a dangerous situation, I am actually safer if I worry about what happens to you.

Emotional and Intellectual Empathy

When we talk about empathy, we usually mean emotional empathy —the ability to feel what another feels.

There are several terms that overlap for this kind of social feeling. *Sympathy* comes from a Greek term meaning "feeling with," and we use it to describe many of the same things we use the word *empathy* for. *Compassion* is the Latin version of *sympathy*: it also means "feeling with." In English, compassion is usually more active than sympathy: we expect someone who has compassion to be doing something about other people's problems.

We also have a kind of intellectual empathy that goes with our emotional empathy. Psychologists call it cognitive empathy, which is related to *an awareness of mind.*

When psychologists talk about an awareness of mind, what they mean is that we look at other people doing things, having reactions to the world around them, and we understand that they are doing these things because there's something going on in their minds. We have thoughts and feelings, and we know that other people have them too.

This isn't as obvious as you might think. Most animals either get along without an awareness of mind or have it in a far less developed state than ours. There's a lot of debate among people who study animal behavior about whether animals other than humans have an awareness of mind, meaning whether they understand that other animals have mental processes like their own. As we see in a lot of these questions about behavior, the answer may not be yes or no but rather somewhere in the middle: some animals have *some aspects* of an awareness of mind.

For example, one study found that some kinds of birds can understand when a competing bird can see the food they both want. Corvids, the group of birds that includes ravens, crows, and jays, are unusually intelligent birds: some of them can make and use simple tools, and they solve problems that require some level of thinking through. They hide bits of food for later, and scientists observed that jays would change the hiding place if they realized they were being watched by another jay. A sophisticated experiment with ravens who had learned to see into another room through a peephole showed that, when they thought they were being observed through the peephole, they would change the way they hid their food, even though they couldn't see the other raven they thought was there. These things suggest an awareness of mind in a limited sense: some birds can understand that the other bird wants the food, too, and they know it even when they can't see the eyeball watching them.[8]

But compare that to the enormous sophistication, complexity, and virtually complete self-reflectivity of our human mental states. We seem to be categorically different. Our sophisticated awareness of mind and our emotional empathy interact. We understand that somebody wants the same food we want. We know that person feels hungry. We know what it's like to feel hunger; we feel it along

---

[8] Thomas Bugnyar, Stephan Reber, and Cameron Buckner, "Ravens Attribute Visual Access to Unseen Competitors," *Nature Communications* 7 (2016): 10506, http://doi.org/10.1038/ncomms10506.

with the other person. We cut the food in half and give one of the halves to the other person.

On the other hand, our awareness of mind can turn against us too. We have to keep reminding ourselves to interpret others' actions with charity because we seem to have a natural tendency to attribute evil motivations to other people. In a state of nature, this could be a useful assumption. We assume that our competitors are trying to steal our food or kick us out of our cave, and we protect ourselves and survive another day. But most of the unpleasantness in our civilized world comes from misunderstanding the motives of others. We never get up and say, "I'll be evil today"—but it's easy for us to imagine other people doing exactly that. Psychologists call these mistakes *attribution bias*: we judge ourselves by a different standard from the one we use to judge others.

When we make these mistakes, we make ourselves angry and miserable. We start to turn off our natural human empathy. Our mistaken intellects turn our emotions against the other. On a personal level, we get into arguments and fights. On a larger scale, we get into wars. "Judge not, that you be not judged" (Matt. 7:1)—good advice from a master of human psychology.

Strangely, our *feelings* of empathy can sometimes lead us to do things that are wrong, even disastrously wrong. We feel sympathy with victims of what we see as an injustice. We get angry along with them. Then we decide we have to do something about it. But we haven't stopped to *think* about the other side of the question. People who join terrorist movements have often been sucked in by this feeling of empathy; because the feeling of anger for the victims of injustice is so strong, they fail to feel empathy for the victims of their terrorist acts.

This is why *cognitive empathy*, as the psychologists call it, is so important. Emotional empathy is the natural feeling we have when we see things happening to other people. Cognitive empathy is the intellectual processing that allows us to put the feelings in perspective and know what to do about them. Psychological experiments suggest that the people who most strongly *feel* empathy with others are not necessarily good at *understanding* other people's mental states.[9] In order to know what to do about our feelings of empathy, we have to be able to understand how other people are likely to be thinking.

Fortunately, we have the equipment for that, in a way that no other creature on earth has.

Think about an Alligator

Here's an easy little science experiment you can do without putting down this book. Are you ready?

Think about an alligator.

Good. Now, what are you thinking about?

An alligator, of course.

But wait a minute. Because I asked what you were thinking about, now you're thinking about thinking about an alligator, aren't you?

Hold on. Now you're thinking about thinking about thinking about an alligator.

This could go on forever, or until we got tired of it, which has probably already happened.

But it's more than just a silly joke. What we just discovered is something that, as far as we know, is uniquely human.

[9] Philipp Kanske et al., "Are Strong Empathizers Better Mentalizers? Evidence for Independence and Interaction between the Routes of Social Cognition," *Social Cognitive and Affective Neuroscience* 11, no. 9 (September 2016): 1383–1392, https://doi.org/10.1093/scan/nsw052.

The Four Levels of Happiness

Some animals can think, in a limited way. We mentioned corvids before: Scientists studying New Caledonian crows have discovered that these birds can solve complex problems in their brains without having to resort to trial and error. These are birds that actually make tools. They're amazingly clever—for birds.

If you live with dogs or cats, you've probably seen some pretty clever problem-solving. I've seen a dog pull a whole tablecloth off a dining room table—and the food with it, of course. That dog was able to figure out how to bring down the food that was out of reach. He was also able to learn that the people were not pleased when he pulled down the tablecloth. I'm not saying he learned to be a better dog, but he did learn to be a sneakier dog.

I think it's fair to call that thinking.

But that loop we just got into with the alligator is something else. As far as we know, humans are the only creatures that can think about thinking. It's a different level of awareness.

Not only do we know that we're thinking, but we also know that other people are thinking. Very young children haven't figured that out yet. They are the centers of their own universes. But they soon begin to understand that their parents, their brothers and sisters, and the other children they meet on the playground are also thinking beings.

Scientists call this the *theory of mind*—the understanding that other people are having thoughts and sensations, just as we are. There's doubt about whether other animals have a theory of mind at all. The evidence seems to suggest that some of the more intelligent animals do have an *awareness of mind* but not a theory of mind—a reflective self-*understanding*. At the very least, human beings have reflective self-understanding to a degree that no other creature comes close to matching. I can think about you reading this book and thinking about me thinking about you—and there's a good chance I've never met you in my life.

There's one more tool we have in dealing with other people. We call it *conscience*, and it's another part of human nature that takes us beyond Levels 1 and 2.

Conscience

Conscience is the built-in sense of right and wrong that we all have.

Now, when I say that we all have a conscience, I have to specify that *all* doesn't *quite* mean "all." There are certain people who don't have a conscience. Sociopaths don't have that faculty, which makes them very dangerous. Instead of a sense of right and wrong, sociopaths have only a sense of "benefits me" and "doesn't benefit me." In order to be fit for society, sociopaths have to be taught to *simulate* a conscience; that is, they have to reason out what a conscience *would* tell them if theirs were in working order. They can sometimes learn to do that by realizing that it will benefit them to be able to function productively in society.

But sociopaths are very rare. Furthermore, it seems that sociopaths are made, not born. Sociopathic children are much rarer than sociopathic adults, and when we do run across one, we can almost always trace the condition to some trauma or brain damage.

For the rest of us, we have a conscience that tells us what's right and wrong. Now, it's not always accurate. Our early training has a lot to do with its decisions. If you grew up in a religious family, religion is probably a big part of what your conscience will be working with, even if you repudiated your religion later. I've known a number of very fine people who considered themselves atheists but lived by obvious Christian values. They gave up on religion—sometimes because of bad things that had happened in their church—but conscience held on to that early training and never let go. It was more a part of them than they realized or cared to admit.

The Four Levels of Happiness

Sometimes a conscience gets distorted by early training. If you grew up in a household that was very much stuck in the default mode of Levels 1 and 2, then your conscience may have been formed by those attitudes. It may strike you as morally wrong not to make the most money possible, even if it means bending other rules to get it. Your conscience may pain you if you fall behind your neighbors and acquaintances in accomplishments or wealth or status. You may have a lot of retraining ahead of you because when you try to move on to the next level of happiness, your conscience will accuse you of neglecting the *important* things. I see that happen a lot to people who grew up in materialist societies—the United States, of course, but also places like Japan or South Korea, where the same sorts of forces work on the conscience from a very young age. You're *supposed* to get ahead in the world. If you're not doing everything you can to get ahead, you're *failing*. If you have that kind of conscience, you're going to need some retraining, and I'd advise you to spend a lot of time with the exercises in this book. They'll help you get your priorities lined up better with what will really make you happy in the long run.

Materialism, of course, isn't the only way conscience can be distorted. Some people can develop a keen sense of social justice, which is a wonderful thing. But all wonderful things can be taken too far—even social justice. There are people who become so obsessed with one idea of social justice that they lose patience with all gradual progress. They become terrorists, and eventually their consciences can be so warped that they feel serious guilt over all the innocent people they haven't killed yet.

Some people fall into crime because that's the world they grew up in. They place loyalty to the gang at the top of their hierarchy of virtues. When you hear about a gang shooting and wonder how people can be so lacking in conscience, you may be asking the wrong question. The murderers may be people with highly developed consciences—but formed in the wrong direction. The need to punish disloyalty ranks so high on their scale of moral imperatives that they would suffer agonies of conscience if they *didn't* murder the gang's enemies.

I doubt whether any gang enforcers are reading this book. But if you are, I'm telling you straight: Your conscience is going to need some work. The good news is that there's work you can do. You can hop off the roller coaster of short-term triumph and long-term misery and find real happiness along with the rest of us.

So we have the *equipment* both to feel along with other people and to understand what they're thinking. And we know that we're built to empathize with others—that we're naturally happier when they're happy and less happy when they're miserable.

But what do we do with that knowledge? In our culture today, everything is geared toward those first two levels of happiness. They're the default setting. How do we escape to Level 3?

6

꒯꒯꒯꒷

Escape to Level 3

Let's take stock of where we are so far. We worked our way through
the first two levels of desire, and we found that they don't lead us
to lasting happiness. They have their good points, but if we stop
there, we're going to be miserable.

The first level is our basic animal instincts—our need for food,
comfort, procreation, and the things that keep us and our species
going. They're absolutely necessary, so we're programmed with
powerful feelings of pleasure if we get them and pain if we don't.
But we're really programmed for a much more uncertain life. In
civilized society, we can indulge our animal desires almost without
limit, and then dopamine homeostasis kicks in and the balance
tilts toward misery.

The second level of desire takes us out of the immediate world
of the senses and makes us work to get ahead of the people around
us. That instinct is probably what made civilization possible,
but it tends to lead us to distorted and unhealthy addictions to
ambition and ego boosting. If we stop at the comparison level
of happiness, we're stuck in an endless loop of anxiety, anger,
and depression.

But there is a higher level of desire than those two, and that
level is where we really begin to see the potential of being human.

In some ways this is like a video game. Each time you level up, you get more power and more ability. We need to go up to the next level to escape the misery of the comparison game. How do we get to Level 3?

It's going to take some work.

Know What You Want

First, we need to be conscious of what we want. This may sound obvious, but it's not really obvious at all. In fact, much of our unhappiness comes from the simple fact that, so far, we've been led by our unconscious desires.

Level 1 operates almost entirely at the preconscious stage of our being. We're programmed to want things automatically, and they're the same things even simple animals want. Food, comfort, sex—these are built-in desires.

In Level 2, we began to have some dealings with the conscious part of our mind. We understand that other people have thoughts and desires, and we compare ourselves to them. We make plans to get ahead of the people around us. We put off immediate pleasures that would fulfill our Level 1 desires, so that we can succeed in satisfying our Level 2 desires.

But we also saw that there's a lot of unconscious stuff going on in Level 2. We develop an unconscious definition of who we are. Are you a winner, a loser, or an in-between? Chances are you didn't think your way to your self-definition there. It just happened, unconsciously. And that unconscious self-definition drives a lot of your behavior. It will end up plotting out the whole course of your life if you let it control your thinking. It will decide what you want your life to be, and it may make a very poor decision.

This is why we need to make a conscious assessment of what we want out of life, and then we must intelligently decide whether we want the right things—the things that will lead to happiness. We're probably going to have some work to do to change our ways of thinking. But it will be worth it if we can escape the cycle of misery that comes from living in the world of Levels 1 and 2.

To help you be conscious of what you want, I'm going to give you four big questions to think about. And I mean *think about*—not answer right away. There's a reason for that, which we'll talk about in a moment. But first the big questions. You may want to write them down or put them in a file on your phone so that you can have them with you wherever you go.

1. What is my purpose in life?
2. How do I think about other people?
3. How do I think of myself?
4. What do I think freedom means?

These four questions will help you figure out where you are on the happiness scale and how much work you have to do to get where you want to be.

There's No Right Answer

Obviously, these aren't easy questions to answer. You might be tempted, psychologically speaking, to give the *right* answer—the answer you think I'd want to hear. Don't do that. There aren't right answers. These are diagnostic questions, not a pop quiz. They're meant to guide you in the right direction for solving your problem. And you already know that you have a problem: you're not as happy as you want to be. That's why you're reading this book.

So, think the questions over, and then set them aside and think about them again. You might want to take the next few days and tell yourself that you'll give ten minutes to thinking about one of the questions every day. You don't have to come up with an answer in those ten minutes. Just think about the question, and let it sink into your mind.

I'm also going to suggest that you keep something handy to record ideas that come to you. Some people keep a notebook in their pockets. Some people dictate memos into their phones. Whatever it takes to be able to record a thought when it comes to you, do that—because that thought might be important, and it's very likely to fade if you don't record it as soon as you think of it.

I suggest having a way to keep notes because this is the way insight often works. We may try to reason through a problem and get nowhere. But don't be surprised if a sudden flash of insight happens in a very unexpected place. You might be in the shower. You might be waiting in line at the Department of Motor Vehicles. You might even be asleep. More than one thorny problem has been solved in a dream.

You may have heard the story of how the structure of DNA was discovered. It was becoming more certain that DNA was what carried the genetic information that makes each of us a unique living thing. But this was a complex protein. How were the parts arranged? One night James Watson had a dream of a spiral staircase. He woke up, and the problem was solved: a double helix, two strands twining around each other.

Dmitri Mendeleev had a similar experience. Writing a chemistry textbook, he began to notice sequences in the elements. Was there some organizing principle in the chemical elements that everyone had missed? His brain kept churning over his observations. Then one night, in a dream, the principle came to him. He saw a table of the elements all laid out in order—the periodic table, as it would come to be known.

The brain, like a sophisticated computer, has background processes going on all the time. If you set yourself a complicated problem, you may not come up with an answer all at once, but if it's important to you, your brain will be working on it at a subconscious level. You're not aware of this work going on in the background, but when that background process has reached an important conclusion, up pops the notification: hey, I found an answer!

So expect insights to come at odd times—in dreams, at work, when you're playing with the dog. Be ready to record those insights somehow. I think it's especially important to have something ready to take notes with beside your bed because dreams are quickly forgotten.

By now you understand that you're going to spend a while thinking about these questions. I'm not going to suggest that you should put aside this book until you have all the answers to them. I know human psychology too well to do that: you're likely to lose your momentum and never pick up the book again, and whatever good you've got from the book will be lost.

But try to be honest with yourself when you answer these questions. I don't just mean you shouldn't give the answers you think I'd want to hear. You shouldn't give the answers you want to hear either. If there's bad news, that's what we're here for: to find a way past our current problems.

So let's talk a little about what you'll find when you answer these questions. Broadly speaking, they'll tell you whether you're dominated by the desires of Level 1 and Level 2, or whether you've started to move on to Level 3 and even Level 4.

1. What Is My Purpose in Life?

When you consider the first question—what is my purpose in life?—try to think not what the purpose of your life *ought* to be but what it actually is right now. Look at your own actions. Try to figure out which things have priority when you're making life decisions. What you do will show you what you actually think.

This may be the hardest question of all. But the world around us is full of easy answers. And all those easy answers are mired in the thinking of Level 1 and Level 2.

You might say that pleasure is the purpose of life. Few people put it so boldly, but many of our answers will amount to saying exactly that. We want to have the things we want when we want them. We want to be comfortable and be able to eat at nice restaurants and have a vacation when we like. If these are the first thoughts that pop into your mind when you think of your purpose in life, that's your instinct talking. You're being dominated by Level 1.

Or you might say that you want to get ahead. Your purpose is to have a good job, to make a lot of money, to get promoted, to be the boss rather than the bossed. That's Level 2 at work. You're thinking in terms of how you compare to the people around you, and you want to be a winner.

But what would it look like if you moved on to the next level?

You might be telling yourself, "My purpose is to make the best contribution I can make. I want my life to make other lives better around me. I want my family to benefit. I want the people I work with to have an easier time. I want my community to be a better place for everybody to live."

If you grew up in America, there's probably something in your brain right now that's saying, "Yeah, *right*."

Because our culture concentrates so much on material accumulation and getting ahead in the comparison game, we start to think that people who seem to desire the good of others just aren't being sincere. There must be something in it for them. It's a scam.

But people who have moved up to the third level of desire—the level where empathy kicks in—have discovered a secret that the people stuck in lower levels can't acknowledge. They know that this apparent selflessness is the escape hatch. It's the door that leads out from the misery of addiction to pleasure and dopamine homeostasis, or the constant anxiety and depression of the comparison game.

And of course, as we've already seen, there's an even higher level than that. You may not be ready to deal with that higher level yet. But it's waiting for you. A person who's gone on to Level 4 desires will begin to say, "My purpose is to bring the Kingdom of God (perfect love) closer on earth." That might even sound silly to you right now. But I think as you get further along in the book, you'll begin to see that you want to be that kind of person.

Now let's go on to the next question, and we'll do the same thing: we'll look at what your answer might tell you about where you fit on the happiness scale.

2. How Do I Think about Other People?

The second question—how do I think about other people?—is broad: it means not just the people around you but also people in other groups, people in other countries, and people in other religions.

Other people can be hard to deal with. The ones around you get in the way a lot. They have wants and desires, and those wants and desires interfere with *your* wants and desires. And those are probably the ones most like you. When different people come in—people from other countries or other religions—they can be even harder to deal with. They speak languages you don't understand. They wear strange clothes. They make the world around you look different, and that can make you uncomfortable.

This is how you know you're still stuck in Levels 1 and 2. The *other* is your enemy, unless the other is your servant. You see other people for what they can do for you, or for what they keep you from gaining for yourself. Other people are generally bad news, and that's what you see in them.

But you could also think that other people make the world worthwhile. Because there are others, you have an opportunity for love. Because there are different kinds of people, you have an opportunity to learn.

I don't mean that you should be indifferent to the differences between religions. I'm a Catholic priest, after all. I think Roman Catholics have the truth in a way that's more complete than anyone else has it. But that doesn't mean I can't learn from other people and other beliefs. Once you move up to that third level, you can see other people as opening opportunities, instead of causing impediments.

So, where are you on that scale? Be honest with yourself. Do you focus on the opportunities or the inconveniences of other people? That will tell you something about what work you have to do.

3. How Do I Think of Myself?

When you consider the third question—how do I think of myself?—don't just answer the way you would if you were telling somebody else the answer. Answer it after serious introspection. Look at what you do and how you set your priorities. What do those things tell you about what you think of yourself?

You may find that your first answer to this question is in terms of how you compare to other people—in other words, whether you're winning or losing.

Do you think about yourself in terms of the money you earn? When you ponder this question, is the first thought that comes to your mind something like, "I'm not earning as much as I could"? If that's what happens, you're making yourself into a thing. You're judging yourself by your value in dollars.

But if you think of yourself first in terms of love—then you've moved up a level. If you say, for example, that you are a good friend or a "good helper"—a loving person—then you've at least made a start on finding your true value. And if you think of yourself as loved and treasured by God—bound for Heaven—then you've come up to that fourth level, the level of transcendence.

4. What Do I Think Freedom Means?

The fourth question—what do I think freedom means?—is one you should spend a good bit of time on. Almost all of us think freedom is a good thing. Our politicians know they can always get applause with that word because there's no one who doesn't want freedom.

But it's just a noise until we know what it means. What do you think of when you hear the word *freedom*? Do you think of not having to do things you don't want to do? Do you think of not being responsible to other people? Do you think of having no commitments you have to honor?

If you're thinking of freedom that way, you'll notice you're consistently thinking of freedom *from* things—freedom from control, freedom from responsibility, freedom from commitment. In this view, commitment seems like a bad thing. It's something you're trying to avoid because it can interfere with what you want to do right now.

But you might be thinking of freedom *for* things instead—freedom to find the deepest meaning in your life; freedom to better love your family and the people around you, and to show that love by doing the things you know will be best for them. This can extend to freedom to make a lifelong commitment to someone or something that's more important than any pleasure or success—a spouse, a family, a cause, a church. Instead of freedom *from*, you think of freedom *for*.

Commitment can be a very good thing if you see freedom this way. Self-sacrifice can be a choice you make, freely, because it leads to deeper and more lasting happiness.

Think about these four questions. Again, it's not a test. It's an exercise to help you understand where you are and where you need to go. So give it some time. Let your mind absorb the questions and give those unconscious mental processes some time to get working.

And keep contemplating while you read these next few chapters, because we're going to tackle each of the questions one at a time and go a lot deeper into them.

7

~~~~

What Is My Purpose in Life?

Once you've been thinking over the first question for a while, you may begin to have a good sense of what your purpose in life has been up to now. By looking at your own priorities, you may be able to say, "Well, really, the thing that's most important to me has always been food." Or you might say, "I've been ambitious, and whenever there's a decision to be made, I put my job and my career prospects first."

It's good to have self-knowledge like that. "Know thyself" is still good advice.

But now that you know the purpose that's actually been driving your thoughts and actions, it's time to think what your purpose *ought* to be. If we really want to reach the next level of happiness—if we want to escape from the miseries of addictive behavior and the comparison game—then what should our priorities be?

To answer this question, we need to think differently. We need to start thinking on that third level, the level where we realize that other people's well-being is essential to our own happiness. So instead of thinking about what would bring us the most immediate pleasure, or how we would be winners in life instead of losers, we need to start thinking about how we can make a positive difference in other people's lives. The strange thing is that this new way of thinking is likely to make our lives more pleasant. It's likely to make us winners in life. But those things happen only because we're willing to set pleasure and winning aside as our main goals. So just forget about that for now and concentrate on understanding that pleasure and winning aren't the highest forms of happiness—but they might be waiting for you at the end of the process anyway as a happy little bonus.

When you ask what *ought* to be your purpose in life, you want to ask not what you can get out of life but what you can put into it. You want to ask how you can do the most good in the world.

Let's break this down into categories. We'll look at the idea of purpose as it affects four different areas of life—four circles, each one wider than the last.

1. Family and Friends

How can I make a positive difference for my family and friends? We start here because these are the people whose happiness you can have the most effect on—and therefore, the people who will affect your happiness the most.

Think about what your life with your family is like. Is there a lot of friction and resentment? Do you find yourself constantly wondering why people in your family aren't living up to your expectations? Do you feel as though they're wondering the same thing about you?

These cycles of resentment and disappointment can go round and round forever. Here's your chance to step off the merry-go-round. Think about what would genuinely do the most good for your family. And don't just think in terms of money. Especially if you're the main breadwinner in the family, that old Level 2 demon, the comparison game, is ready to start whispering in your ear, "What you could do for your family is bring in more cash." But money isn't likely to lead to happiness. I don't mean that you should ignore the money question completely. I don't want you to be irresponsible and leave the future to fend for itself. But I do think you should be looking somewhere else when you try to answer the question "What can I do that would bring the *most* benefit to my family?"

The same is true with your friends—and even more so, because most of the time your friends aren't relying on you for money. Look at the way your relationships with your friends work. Do you think you're doing what you ought to be doing to be a good friend? What would that even look like?

I'd include people you work with closely when you're thinking about how to make a positive difference in your friends' lives. How can you make their lives easier and happier? How can you help them have more of what they need for their own happiness?

Think about these things over and over. As ideas come to you, write them down or keep notes on your phone or whatever you've decided to do to keep track of them. After a while, you'll probably see a list starting to form after this question. Meanwhile, let's go on to the next circle.

2. Work

How can I make a positive difference where I work? You might work for a huge tech company with offices all over the globe. Or you might work in a little store on a back street that sells quilting supplies. Maybe you work as an independent contractor at home. But if you're like most people, work is where you spend a lot of your time, maybe most of your time. So it's going to have to be a big part of your thinking when you're trying to move up in the scale of happiness—all the more because many workplaces, like schools, encourage us to compare ourselves to the people around us and see whether we're winning or losing.

The Four Levels of Happiness

This is the kind of thinking you should avoid when you're mulling over this aspect of the question. You're not going for the employee-of-the-month plaque here. You want to make a real contribution, *even if nobody notices*. What things can you do that would most improve life for the people you work with? That includes the other employees if you work for a company, or that company's customers and suppliers, or your clients if you're self-employed – all the people who depend on you for the work you do.

You might discover that there's a lot of tension where you work. That's normal in an environment where getting ahead is what people expect to do. What can you do to reduce the tension?

Maybe you can be a force for calm. Just being friendly will start to change the people around you. You have more control than you realize over how your encounters with other people go. Psychologically, it's hard for other people to resist a friendly approach. Even the ones you think of as constitutionally nasty will have a hard time snapping at you if you come to them with a smile. And if they do snap at you, then you can just assume that the next encounter will go better and reset. You'll find that the people who seem miserable and cranky have a surprising capacity for cheerfulness if you help them bring it out. Not holding on to resentments may be one of the most useful things you can do for your colleagues at work.

Aside from the individual people, what can you do for the organization as a whole? Whether it's a tiny storefront business or a multinational tech empire, you have your part to play in its success. And we're not defining success with just money here. In the business world, it's easy to think in terms of this quarter's numbers and stop there. But any organization needs more than a good quarter, or even a string of good quarters, for long-term success. It needs employees who will do their best. It needs customers who believe they'll get what they need from the company and who trust the people in the company to do their best work. It needs suppliers and contractors who trust that dealing with this company is worth some extra work to keep its business. All those things don't happen overnight: they're a product of the *culture* of the organization, and the culture is exactly what you can influence every day.

So, when you ask yourself what you can do for your organization (even if your organization is only you), think about all these things. Ask yourself what you can be doing now to make the long-term prospects better. You'll be coming up with answers that will direct you toward your purpose in this category.

3. The Community, Culture, and Society

How can I make a positive difference in the community, the culture, and society as a whole? I put those three things together, but I put them in that particular order because I think you have to start at the smallest level. It's great to have a vision of all of Western culture becoming enlightened and embracing the way of charity and truth, but it will probably remain a vision in your lifetime.

I've heard people lately use *incrementalism* as a dismissive term, as if it were a bad thing to work for change a bit at a time, instead of doing away with all bad things all at once, right now. But I notice those people haven't changed things. They're still complaining about the things that need to be changed. That's because incrementally is the only way to get anything important accomplished. You might say, "I don't want to *practice* the piano. I want to play Beethoven right now." But you can't, because you need to put in some incremental work before you get to the *Appassionata*. That incremental work is rewarding too—playing simpler things while you work up to Beethoven sonatas is rewarding in itself. But you can't skip straight to perfect concert pianist.

The same point is true when you want to change elements in society. If you try to wipe out everything bad and start from scratch, what you end up with is the French Revolution. And that only leads to another French Revolution (and then an empire, and then a royalist restoration, and then a different monarchy, and then a republic, and then an empire . . .).

Yet incremental change is real change, and the small changes pile up. Look at the civil rights movement. Have we built a world of perfect equality yet? Certainly not. But in my lifetime we've gone from a country where racial segregation was the law in many states, and the de facto standard in most of the rest, to a country where equality is the law and people younger than me have to read about Jim Crow in history books. We've made enormous changes by making one small adjustment after another. We shouldn't let the fact that we're not yet perfect blind us to those accomplishments.

Now, what does that tell you about your own situation? I think it tells you that even the little things you do in your community really matter.

Let's imagine that there's a retaining wall on your street, and one night some kids spray graffiti on it. That makes all your neighbors feel worse about the neighborhood every time they pass the wall, even though it was probably just some kids on a dare. What can you do?

Well, it's a city-owned wall, so you can call the city department of public works or the mayor's suggestion hotline, or some other department, and see if you can find someone who will put your street's wall on the schedule for maintenance sometime in the future.

Or you can take a little paint chip from the wall, go down to the hardware store, match the color, and get together with a couple of neighbors. You can make that graffiti disappear in ten minutes.

Just a little thing—but it improves the quality of life for everybody. Maybe even for the kids who spray-painted the graffiti.

I think you should imagine yourself doing things like that—small activities and adjustments that improve life in your own neighborhood, even though they don't take up a whole lot of your time. Then you can go on to thinking about how you'll have a positive effect on culture.

We love to complain about our culture today. Our entertainment is full of pornography and violence. Our conversation is full of vulgarity. But what can we do? That's what the culture is like.

Well, one thing we can do is not participate in the bad parts of our current culture. If you think a movie is going to be irresponsibly violent, then don't watch it. Do you find that your own conversation is filling up with curse words because that's the way people talk these days? Well, you don't have to be one of those people. No one forces you to use offensive language. But it does become a habit. You could do your part to make our culture better by making a conscious effort to change the way you talk. Remember what Gandhi said about being the change you want to see in the world? This was what he was talking about. You change your own behavior, and you've made a difference already.

Maybe you have more influence than that. Are you a creative type? Do you have a lot of followers on social media? You can lead them in the direction you want to see our culture going. I don't mean you have to lecture them. Just be yourself, but better—better than you would be if you didn't have a vision of a better culture in mind.

Think about all these considerations, write down ideas as they come to you, and you'll have more of an answer when you ask yourself what your purpose in life is.

All the same principles apply to your contribution to society as a whole. No one is going to knock on your door and tell you that you've been made dictator for life. (And you'd get tired of that job soon enough anyway.) So you're not going to be able to point out the problems in society, order them to be solved, and then relax and take it easy. But you can make your own contribution that will make society as a whole better.

What will it be? Will you get involved in politics? I don't necessarily wish that on you, but if you have the talent for it, that's one way you can help the rest of us. Or do you have a particular interest or talent that the rest of us really need? We can all use better medical care. We can all use safer transportation.

But you may already know by this time what you're going to do to improve society as a whole. Chances are, if you've started working on the changes you were going to make in the other areas of your life, you're already improving society as a whole. The important thing is to find that sense of purpose you need in a realistic and achievable way.

4. Church and the Kingdom of God

How can I make a positive difference to my church and the Kingdom of God? There may be some eye-rolling going on right now, and that's okay. But I've already warned you that I think you need to acknowledge the transcendent—the world beyond the senses—if you're going to complete your journey toward happiness.

If you already have faith or participate in a church, think about how you might make the best possible contribution to that church as well as the people around you: How can you help them grow in faith and come closer to the transcendent or to the loving God? Inasmuch as your faith helps you view others as transcendent mysteries—as little eternities destined for fulfillment by a deity who is perfect love, goodness, truth, beauty, and being—what might you do to help them fulfill their ultimate purpose in life?

If you do not have faith, keep yourself open to the possibility as we explore this concept further in this book. When you consider that so many studies show that religion—or at least faith in the transcendent—is so important to human happiness,[10] why not keep an open mind?

[10] See the references in footnote 52 in chapter 17.

8

~~~~~

How Do I Think about Other People?

Starting to think more deeply about the people around you is where the third level really distinguishes itself from the other two.

So far we've been talking about what *we* want—what we think our purpose in life should be. At the third level, we've started to realize that we want to be and do things that make us better and happier. That's a big step forward.

But now, we turn to others. And since we've started thinking beyond the default modes of desire, we begin to see those others with very different eyes.

When we were running on our Level 2 desires, we asked how we compared to others and whether we were *winning*. That predisposed us to think of the other as the rival.

Now we're thinking on a higher level, and we want to think about what's *good* about those other people we deal with every day. Our natural sense of empathy is trying to teach us that others' happiness affects our own. But our default ways of thinking can be a roadblock to that understanding. We need to get over them.

So, once again, we're going to do some contemplation. There will be a series of questions, but you shouldn't just run down the list and write down the first answers that come to you. Instead, think about these questions for fifteen minutes or so every day.

Again, it may work best if you set aside a particular time when you don't have to do anything but sit and think. I know that's hard, especially for Americans, because we always want to be accomplishing something. But, believe me, this contemplation is accomplishing something. You just can't see it right away, but it will sneak up on you.

Sit in a quiet place (if you can find one) and think about the people you deal with every day. You might want to focus on one in particular right now. Then start asking yourself a few questions:

1. What good deeds do these people try to do?
2. What little acts of kindness do they do that they didn't have to do?
3. What little quirks do they have that I really enjoy?
4. How are they trying to be my friends?
5. What are their values?
6. What are their aspirations in life?
7. What strengths do they have that complement my strengths?
8. What religious commitments do they have?

1. The Good Deeds of Others

What good deeds do the people around me try to do? It's a little harder than you'd think to look at other people this way. Psychological research (and your own experience) has shown that we assess others' motivations differently from our own. When we do something, we convince ourselves that what we're doing is good and right, or at least reasonable. We don't usually get up in the morning and think, "I'll bet I can really put one over on Fred today. I'll bet I can show Lucy how much better I am than she is."

But we imagine other people doing exactly that sort of thing. Psychologists have found that there is an asymmetry in the way we attribute motivations: for the same action, we're more likely to attribute *good* motives to ourselves and *bad* motives to someone else.

So, what we're trying to do now is reverse that asymmetry. We're training ourselves in *cognitive* empathy. What we want to do is see the other person from the inside, as much as that's possible, and try to imagine what that other person thinks.

When you start thinking this way, you'll begin to observe that some of the actions other people take are things they do because they want to be good. These may even be things that annoy you, but the people around you aren't doing them to annoy you. They're doing them because they think these acts are the right things to do.

You may have to revise your opinion of somebody completely once you start thinking this way. You'll be on the lookout for the *good* that person does, and you may find it unexpectedly.

For example, suppose you go out for lunch with your friend Greg from work every Tuesday. Every time it's his turn to pay, he always counts his change carefully, and you think to yourself that he must be a tightwad to be that fussy with his money. Then one day—after you've been trying to notice the good things about Greg for a while—you watch him count his change, and he suddenly walks back to the cashier and hands back a dollar he wasn't entitled to. Now you have a different way of looking at Greg's habit. Maybe he's not a tightwad after all. Maybe he has a strong sense of justice, even in the little things, and it bothers him at least as much to get a buck he wasn't supposed to get as it does to be shortchanged. He's trying to be a good person, according to his notions of what good people do.

2. The Acts of Kindness of Others

What little acts of kindness do the people around me do that they didn't have to do? This is another case where we have to be observant.

The Four Levels of Happiness

Some people go out of their way to do a random act of kindness in a showy way—like paying for a meal for the next person in line at the fast-food joint. Now, when I say *showy*, I don't mean that's necessarily a bad thing at all. It's good to let people see there's kindness in the world, and I enjoy seeing it when it's on display.

But for others, you may have to be a little more observant.

Why does Bennett always park at the far end of the lot every single day? Maybe it's because he's trying to leave the nearer spaces for people who are older and less mobile than he is.

Why does Jazmeen always check the coffeepot when she walks by the break room, even when she's not getting coffee for herself? Maybe it's to see whether it needs filling again, because she wants to be sure that everyone will have coffee when they want it.

Once you start thinking about the acts you've observed people doing during the day, you may begin to realize that a lot of people are just trying to be nice. They want to do something kind, because being kind makes them feel good, and it makes them feel as though they've done something to make the world just a little bit better.

3. The Enjoyable Little Quirks of Others

What little quirks do the people around me have that I really enjoy? This is a little more complicated, but it's getting closer to the heart of what it really means to move up to Level 3. In our first two questions, we talked about what other people are trying to do to be good or be nice. That at least partly judges them by what makes them beneficial to us—in other words, by what good we get out of them. But now we want to see them for who they are themselves, independent of any benefit we might be getting. This is getting to the heart of Level 3: other people delight us not just because they do good things for us but because of who they are in themselves. Their differences from us and their unique goodness and delightfulness enlighten, enliven, and complement us. Their mere presence elicits satisfaction, goodwill, and friendship.

For example, maybe you know someone from India who speaks perfect English, but English as she learned it in India. It has a different rhythm and a different lilt. She uses phrases and metaphors you understand perfectly but that you would never have come up with yourself. She sees life differently, and you enjoy just hearing her talk because no one else around you produces that kind of music with their voice. It's a difference that doesn't make your life better in any material way, but your life is more delightful because she's part of it.

Or you might know someone who collects stamps and has stories about stamp-collecting triumphs. You might know nothing about stamps yourself, but you look forward to the stories because your friend's friendship and enthusiasm come across, and he tries to make the stories interesting to you. You don't benefit in any material way, but you feel as though the world is better because you can experience some of his joy and enthusiasm.

People are different, and at Levels 1 and 2 those differences can annoy us. They just get in our way. But as we move up to Level 3, we begin to see the differences in a new light. We begin to see that the differences are why there *are* other people in the first place. Their uniquely good and delightful presence makes us come alive in new ways—and our unique goodness and delightfulness do the same for them.

4. Efforts Others Make to Be My Friends

How are the people around me trying to be my friends? Of course, not everyone will want to be your friend. Some people—even good and pleasant individuals—may just not like you. You'll be surprised how few of those people are out there, but it could happen. Others just may not have any common interests. But open yourself up to the possibility that people are sending you friendship signals.

You do that yourself, don't you? Maybe without even thinking about it, you let it be known that you wouldn't mind getting to know someone better.

Some of these signals can be overt. Someone might ask you if you want to have lunch together to talk more about that point you were discussing in the break room. That's clear enough.

But other signals can be more subtle than that. They may be signals the other person isn't even aware of sending. It may be that someone always has something to say when you pass in the hall—something more than just "good morning." Or it may be that someone makes a point of directing your attention to a concert she thinks you'll be interested in.

Friendship is in an odd position in our current culture. We don't quite know what to do with it. We talk so much about sex that we sometimes think that any clear offer of friendship must be a romantic overture. But friendship is a different bond, a different type of relationship, one that is beautiful and valuable. As you contemplate this question, you may begin to realize that there are people who would be happy to be your friends, people you would enjoy getting to know better. How are you responding to those signals that they would be happy to be your friends? How *should* you be responding?

We have a finite amount of time and psychic energy, so we can't be "best friends" with everybody. We must choose carefully which friends we can best support and who can best support us. Nevertheless, we can be hospitable, neighborly, and even helpful and supportive when time and resources permit. These kinds of friendships enhance and enliven both others and ourselves, making us happier.

5. The Values of Others

What are the values of the people around me? To a surprising degree, people have the same basic values. We talked about that when we talked about conscience: we all believe murder is wrong, for example.

But different people have different priorities, and as you think about the individuals you know, you'll begin to see that what they say and what they do demonstrate those priorities. We can say that the items you place at the top of your priority list are your *values* in the most literal sense: they're the elements you think are most valuable because you're willing to give up other things for them.

So think about someone you know. What does that person value most?

You might see that it's family. If the person you're thinking of gives up other good things to care for a sick child or visit a grand-parent in a nursing home, you see the person's values in action. Family means something more to that person than it means to many other people.

For someone else, the dominant value might be religion. If you have a friend who goes to daily Mass no matter what, who's always organizing parish activities, who takes time off work or postpones vacations to be available when the church needs him, that's a person who puts religion high up on the scale of values.

It's not hard to work out most people's values by observing them like this. But there is one point we have to beware of. Remember what we discovered about motivation: that we tend to attribute better motivations to ourselves and worse motivations to others. It may be tempting to watch other people and degrade their values to something less attractive. We might see someone who often stays late at work and think, "Well, she's greedy and ambitious." But she might say that she values hard work and that she hates to leave her colleagues in the lurch when there's a deadline coming up. Try to see it from her point of view. What do you think *she* sees as the motive behind her behavior? That will tell you what her values are. And ignore that cynical part of your brain that wants to degrade those values to lower-level desires.

6. The Life Aspirations of Others

What are the life aspirations of the people around me? Look beyond what people want to accomplish in their careers. You might say, "He wants to be director of marketing," and you could be right. But many people have bigger aspirations than that. It's true, especially in America, that we tend to let ambition take the top spot in our desires. But in their imaginations, most people have some great good they would like to accomplish, an endeavor that would make the world better. Maybe someone you know really cares about poverty and hunger. Maybe someone else really loves his city and has a vision for your hometown that would make it a more beautiful place to live. These points are worth noticing because they give us a glimpse of the good things inside that other person's mind.

So spend some time trying to imagine someone else's ideal world. You may be surprised how much it looks like your ideal world. This is especially valuable if it's someone you disagree with politically, because in politics our natural instinct to attribute evil motives to others bubbles to the tops of our minds very quickly. But if you can understand that you share a vision of how the world should be, and just have a disagreement about how to get there, then you've established a point of sympathy, a way of thinking that you share.

7. The Complementary Strengths of Others

What strengths do the people around me have that complement my strengths? This will require an honest assessment of your strengths as well as other people's, and honestly assessing your own strengths isn't always easy. But it's worth doing. You probably already know some tasks you're good at or skills you have that other people can make use of. You might enjoy woodworking, for example, or you might be good at solving computer problems. Now, think about some of the other people you know. What can they do? Maybe you know someone who likes to paint. Maybe there's an artistic-furniture partnership in your future.

Once you start to think of other individuals' strengths, you'll discover that people have much more to offer than just mechanical talents, as useful as those are. You might know someone who's very patient, for example. Or you might know someone who has an instinctive understanding of how to get along with people. Maybe you're not all that good at the people part yourself, but you have a talent for music, and you love to play for an audience. One of you could be the organizer and the other the musician for neighborhood events.

As you contemplate more, think about more than utility. Maybe you have a love of philosophy, and someone you know is deeply moved by art. Those are two routes to the Divine, and you might find that sharing your passions will lead you both further than you could have gone alone.

8. The Religious Commitments of Others

What religious commitments do the people around me have? For some, the answer will be none at all. But a majority of people consider themselves religious. What does that mean to the person you're thinking of?

For some people, it's easy to find obvious religious commitments. If your friend goes to Mass every day, you know that's someone who's deeply dedicated to the Catholic Church. If someone has to take regular breaks to pray facing Mecca, you know that's a person who takes Islam seriously.

But you'll meet a lot of people who don't belong to what we call an "organized religion" and yet consider themselves committed to the spiritual. I think they're missing something vital, as we'll talk about later on. But they're sincere, and their beliefs are important to them. What are those beliefs? You might discover some of them by what they say, but you'll also see some of them in what they do. Are certain rituals and traditions important to them? Do they have certain definite ideas about what they should and shouldn't do, ideas that they might not even be able to explain but that guide them when they make decisions?

Again, don't just observe. Try to understand from the inside. Try to imagine why the people you're thinking about do the things they do and believe the things they believe, and try to understand why those beliefs are good. You may find yourself admiring those people and wishing you could be more like them. Great! You're really getting somewhere.

And, as you've noticed, we're peeking ahead toward the fourth level we identified earlier on — the level of the transcendent, where we start to take into account more than the material things we feel and see. So let's continue in that direction for just a little while.

What Is Revealed by Our Transcendental Desires?

To understand what is revealed by our transcendental desires, let's start with the idea of desire. When we have a desire for something, it's usually because it's necessary for us. We have a desire for food because the individual can't continue without food. We have a desire for procreation because the species can't continue without procreation. So when we have a desire for something beyond the material, it's reasonable to say that it's something we're designed to desire because we need it.

What are these transcendental desires? In a phrase, they are the desire for ever-greater truth, ever-greater love, ever-greater fairness or justice, and ever-greater beauty. As we shall see, these desires go beyond the physical world and beyond materiality itself, and they imply a transcendent reality inciting them within our consciousness. That's quite a leap—and we will discuss the evidence for it below.

These transcendental desires are almost universal, and they lie at the heart of both Western and Eastern philosophy. They also describe four of the seven common characteristics of major world religions.[11] In the West, philosophers in the ancient world (such as Plato and Aristotle), the medieval world (such as St. Augustine and St. Thomas Aquinas), and the contemporary world (such as Alfred North Whitehead, Jacques Maritain, and Bernard Lonergan), all of whom started their own schools of philosophy, believed that these transcendental desires are central not only to metaphysics (which attempts to explain the whole of reality) but also to philosophical anthropology and human existence itself.

Now let's get to the evidence for these transcendental desires. I know the forthcoming material will be difficult for some readers to understand, but I would ask you to be patient and to be satisfied even with a partial understanding. I think it will be worth it because it reveals our transcendental nature as well as the existence of transcendent reality itself (a reality beyond the physical world and materiality itself).

[11] See Friedrich Heiler, "The History of Religions as a Preparation for the Cooperation of Religions," in *The History of Religions*, ed. Mircea Eliade and Joseph Kitagawa (Chicago: Chicago University Press, 1959), 142–144.

The Four Levels of Happiness

A. What Is Revealed by Our Desire for Ever-Greater Truth?

When we look at our family members and friends, we probably notice that they are seeking some form of higher truth about other people, the world, and perhaps the whole of reality. Some people, like myself, are very interested in science, logic, and philosophy, which always seems to lead to greater and greater horizons of reality—far beyond our world, our universe, and even multiverses. The more we explore, the greater reality seems to be. Our exploration reveals not only greater horizons of reality around us but also greater horizons of reality within us.

Sir Arthur Eddington, one of the greatest physicists and cosmologists who ever lived, put it this way:

> We all know that there are regions of the human spirit untrammeled by the world of physics. In the mystic sense of the creation around us, in the expression of art, in a yearning towards God, the soul grows upward and finds the fulfillment of something implanted in its nature. The sanction for this development is within us, a striving born with our consciousness or an Inner Light proceeding from a greater power than ours. Science can scarcely question this sanction, for the pursuit of science springs from a striving which the mind is impelled to follow, a questioning that will not be suppressed. Whether in the intellectual pursuits of science or in the mystical pursuits of the spirit, the light beckons ahead and the purpose surging in our nature responds.[12]

What Eddington is trying to say here is that our continuous striving for greater scientific knowledge is like our striving for

---

[12] Sir Arthur Eddington, *The Nature of the Physical World* (Cambridge: Cambridge University Press, 1958), 327–328.

greater perfection in art, justice, and even the spiritual life. It's like a light within our nature that beckons us ahead, and for scientists, artists, and mystics alike, it is irresistibly drawing us ever closer to its higher power and mind.

Perhaps you, your family members, or friends are not as fascinated by science, but rather by people and trying to understand what makes them tick—to get to the whole truth about them. You may have noticed that the more you discover about people, the wider and deeper the horizon of knowledge becomes. Like in the sciences, the human psyche seems to invite not only greater curiosity but greater discovery—and with that discovery, a greater human mystery. Might Eddington's light be beckoning the studiers of people in the same way as scientists? Might it be revealing itself within every human being?

As we gaze upon our family members and friends, we will probably discover that they are interested in a huge variety of subjects, but the one characteristic most of them probably have in common is that they want to continue questioning unceasingly in areas where they have particular interests until they have reached the *whole* truth. Since this striving is unique to human beings and will endlessly seek what is beyond itself until it gets to the *whole* truth, we might conclude that we are *transcendent* beings—not limited to this world, not limited to physical reality—beings that will be satisfied only with the knowledge of everything about everything: *perfect* truth.

When we gaze upon our fellow men and women striving for the beyond, we might recall the words of St. Augustine at the beginning of his *Confessions*: "For you have made us for yourself, and our hearts are restless until they rest in you."[13]

[13] Augustine, *Confessions* 1.1.

B. *What Is Revealed by Our Desire for Ever-Greater Love?*

Now let's shift our focus from pursuing higher levels of truth to pursuing higher levels of love. If you have moved your focus from Level 1 and Level 2 happiness to Level 3 happiness, then you are likely to be animated and excited by making an optimal contribution to as many people as possible. And if you have moved to Level 4 happiness, then you are likely to be animated by contributing not only to others but also to God and His kingdom.

Have you ever wondered why contributing to someone else or to God makes *you* happy? As we have said before, this shift from Levels 1 and 2 to Levels 3 and 4 improves our lives by alleviating the negative and dark emotions of the comparison game. But is this the whole reason? When most of us make the decision to shift from aggrandizing ourselves to contributing to others and God, we probably didn't do so only to escape the miseries of the comparison game—at least not consciously. So why do we do it? What is it we are trying to get to?

If I think about my own journey, I'd attribute this shift to the satisfaction that comes from getting to know others and enhancing their lives. There seems to be no end to the fascinating, delightful, and good transcendental mysteries that surround me. As with seeking the truth, I seem to know that almost *every* human being is a transcendent mystery deserving of respect, empathy, support, and love. This awareness of the intrinsic goodness, lovability, and transcendence of virtually *every* human being is like Eddington's light beckoning ahead. It not only incites us to empathy with others but draws us into deeper relationships with them—almost endlessly.

Is our striving for ever-greater empathy and relationship connected with our striving for ever-greater truth? If so, then Eddington's "light that beckons ahead" may be the common source.

This implies once again that we are transcendent mysteries—never content with the "here and now" but in ceaseless pursuit of perfect love as well as perfect truth.

C. What Is Revealed by Our Desire for Ever-Greater Fairness or Justice?

Most people would like to be treated as fairly as possible. Very few, except masochists, would wish to be treated unfairly. Curiously, many of us also want to treat others fairly. This may explain why the Silver Rule—the most fundamental principle of justice—has been acknowledged as good by almost every culture and religion in history. The Silver Rule goes like this: "Do not do unto others what you would not have them do unto you." It may be restated as "Don't do avoidable harms to others that you don't want done to you."

We follow this rule not simply to avoid being harmed by others —"I better not harm others too much; otherwise they may harm me back"—but to fulfill a genuine desire. This desire goes beyond avoiding unnecessary harms: it seeks *fair* treatment for others. Fairness includes giving people what is owed to them, not taking things that belong to them, and assuring that they are not reduced to a miserable state of existence. So it seems that our peace of mind and contentment are somehow wrapped up in *other* people's fair treatment.

Many political philosophers, such as Niccolò Machiavelli and Thomas Hobbes, disagreed with this, asserting that most people are fundamentally driven by selfishness to get whatever they can, even by being incredibly unfair. As we have seen, not all people are like this. Though Level 1 and 2 individuals might say, "I carry my own weight—you should too!" Level 3 and 4 people really want others to be treated fairly, and if they are not, they feel almost as badly as being unfairly treated themselves.

The Four Levels of Happiness

Some Level 3 and 4 people go further: they want to optimize fairness as much as possible in just about every walk of life—from the legal system to the political system to the educational system and beyond. They do it not to gain something for themselves but to gain better lives and a better world for as many as possible.

Where does this desire come from? It seems to share something in common with the other transcendental desires because it incites us to ceaselessly go *beyond* our current reality until we have reached a perfect ideal. In this case, the ideal we are seeking is perfect fairness and justice for others, the community, the culture, the state, and even the world.

Inasmuch as our desire for ever-greater fairness or justice is similar to or connected with our desire for ever-greater truth and ever-greater love, its source may again be likened to Eddington's light that beckons ahead. If so, then our desire for ever-greater fairness or justice, like our desires for ever-greater truth and love, implies that we are transcendental beings. Thus, we are not just material stimulus-response machines but transcendent realities continuously striving for the good, not only for individuals but for every societal group and for every social system and organization.

D. What Is Revealed by Our Desire for Ever-Greater Beauty?

Most of us seek greater and greater experiences of beauty. If a musical piece is beautiful, we try to make it louder to intensify its effect on us. If a garden is beautiful, we keep trying to make it just a little bit better—cultivating it in different ways, moving plants and flowers. We also try to make our houses more beautiful, our clothes more beautiful, and ourselves more beautiful. Curiously, we want the "more beautiful" not only for ourselves but also in every experience of nature, art, architecture, music, mathematics, science, and metaphysics, and even in the spiritual.

Though many Level 1 and 2 individuals want to *possess* beautiful things, Level 3 and 4 people are generally content to appreciate, contemplate, and share what is beautiful—whether it be in a museum, a church, nature, or their living rooms.

Inasmuch as beauty evokes a sense of joy, awe, inspiration, mystery, and even the mystical, we might say that beauty lifts our spirit to greater and greater heights. This soaring of spirit does not stop at the boundaries of worldly or human forms. It seems to press onward toward a transcendent beauty that many artists, musicians, and theologians have called glorious, magnificent, majestic, and awe-inspiring.

Once again, we see that our desire for beauty shares something in common with our desire for truth, love, and fairness or justice: it ceaselessly seeks an ever-greater sense of an ideal that will only rest when it has found completeness and perfection. In this case, it is seeking ever more inspiring and resplendent forms of music, architecture, and art, which are directed toward a transcendent ideal. This is probably why Eddington included beauty and art, along with science, spirit, and the mystical, in his "light that beckons ahead."

E. Conclusion to Section 9

We have seen Eddington's "light that beckons ahead" in our unceasing striving for a perfect ideal in truth, love, fairness/justice, and beauty—an ideal that is beyond ourselves and even our universe. Eddington recognized that this light is beyond the material world and, therefore, a transcendent spiritual reality. If he was correct, this reality would mean, once again, that we are not mere stimulus-response machines but transcendent mysteries that are meant for much more than anyone or anything in this world can fulfill. We are reflections of transcendent reality itself.

Can we demonstrate the existence of Eddington's light within our consciousness more conclusively? If so, it would be one of the greatest insights known to humankind — one that would positively affect not only our conception of self but also our conception of human nature, the world, and the whole of reality, including the transcendent itself. This insight would transform not only our happiness but the way we treat one another — and what we consider to be the true purpose and dignity of our lives. We will devote much of chapter 11 to the demonstration of this sublime truth.

Conclusion to Chapter 8

The overall goal of all these questions is to start thinking *good* thoughts about the people around you. Fill your mind with the qualities about them that are positive, that are admirable, endearing, and transcendent. You'll begin to see the other individuals in your life as valuable *for themselves*, not for what they can do for you, and not as rivals to be passed by or squashed. That's when you've made a big step up out of the quagmire of the comparison game.

Once you've tuned your perceptions to the positive side of other people, *imagine* yourself acting on that perception. You may find that you're already doing things differently. Just seeing how people's actions have a good motivation, how their needs and desires are like ours, how the transcendent inner light makes their goodness more evident, enables us to live together more positively. Now you can start thinking about what you would do to make their lives better. And that would make your life better because, as John Donne would tell you, we are inextricably interrelated with and caught up in the lives of one another.

Once again, the power of imagination will go to work in your mind, enabling you to better accomplish your goals. Imagine the friendships you could enter into. Imagine the tasks you could accomplish with someone else whose positive attributes are good complements to your own.

There's another good reason for observing the people around you. I almost hesitate to mention it because it sounds selfish. But it's a fact that friendships and relationships will go better with people who are at the same level on the happiness ladder that you're on.

In fact, this book isn't meant to be a marriage manual. But if you were choosing a spouse rationally, you'd want to take a realistic assessment of that person's progress, and a realistic assessment of your own, into account.

The reason is probably obvious when you think about it. Suppose you're someone dominated by Level 2 desires. Your world is defined by competition and ambition. You think getting ahead is important. Now suppose you marry someone who exists at that third level, the level of empathy. What's going to happen? You're not going to understand each other very well. You'll have constantly conflicting goals. You'll wonder why your spouse doesn't care as much as you about your career, about bringing in more money, about making a good showing in the neighborhood. Your spouse will wonder why you seem to be so heartless, why you don't care about other people, why you put work ahead of family all the time. You're not going to have an easy relationship.

The same is true if you've reached Level 4 and your spouse is at Level 3. It might be easier, but you'll still have conflicts. You'll wonder why your spouse doesn't seem to care about the religious side of life. Your spouse will wonder why you insist on going to church when it's a beautiful day for a picnic with the family. There will be resentments.

And the same is true with friendships, though at least friends don't have to live together most of the time, and so they can take long breaks apart. But still, you'll have trouble matching your priorities. You'll be heading in different directions, and the ties that bind you will fray.

So there are good, sound, practical reasons why you might want to observe where the people you see every day are on the happiness ladder.

But the much greater point is that you get to know them as people. That's the real goal of this stage of the process. Now we can go on to the next set of questions, but if I'm right, you're happier already.

9

How Do I Think of Myself?

When you stop to reflect on what you think of yourself, it's a trickier consideration than it sounds. What do you think of the nose on your face? It's right there, but you can't see it, or at least not more than part of it—unless you stand in front of a mirror.

These next few questions are designed to be your mirror. Stand in front of them, and try to describe what you see.

1. Empathy

What do I think of empathy? Is that something I try to develop in myself? It's easy to give a thoughtless answer to this question. The temptation is to say, "Well, I'm full of empathy, and everything would be fine if other people weren't such jerks."

But you have to be honest with yourself because you're trying to move past whatever it is that's been standing in the way of your happiness. So if you find yourself thinking that most of the people around you are jerks, you should probably answer no to this question.

2. Humility

Am I humble? We'll talk more about humility later when we come to the fourth level. But right now, the important point to know about humility is that it's essential for getting along with other people. Humility means not thinking you're better than the rest of the people around you.

3. Treatment of Others

How do I treat other people? This is a broad question, but I think you can answer it honestly by looking at the broad patterns of your life. Do you often find that people are annoyed with you for what seems like no good reason? It may be because they see something in your behavior toward them that you don't see. Try to imagine what it might be. Are you patient, kind, loyal, and willing to give people your time? These are the qualities that really show other people how you feel about them.

4. Priorities

If I think empathy, humility, and considerate treatment of others are important, do I think they're more important than my career, or my bank account, or my status, or how I look? If the answer is no, then your priorities probably need an adjustment. How will you know what the answer is? One way is to imagine a hypothetical situation in which you could get ahead in your career, for example, by giving up a friendship. Would you decide that your career was important enough to do that?

5. Virtue Valuation

How much do I value virtue? Virtue is a word that may provoke snickers in our modern culture. But it's one of the components of happiness. Is honesty important to you? Not just emotional honesty—telling people how you really *feel*, which is fashionable these days—but honesty that actually costs you something, like taking responsibility for a failure at work. Do you have a strong sense of fairness to others, even if it means you have to give up something of your own? Do you try to practice self-discipline, or are you blown by the winds of appetite and comparison?

6. The Transcendent

Finally, where do I stand in relation to the transcendent? Do you consider the spiritual part—your relationship with the Divine—the most important part of your life? Or do you deny it altogether? Or do you set it aside as something that's nice to think about once in a while but not one of your big priorities? And if you do consider it the most important part of your life, how do you let that fact guide the rest of what you do? The answer to this question is important because—as I've already said—I think your happiness will depend on it. You need to know where you are now so that you can know what work you have to do. And if you don't believe there is such a thing as a spiritual world—well, you'll hear more arguments for it in a little while, but that's your answer to the question for the moment.

Once again, don't try to answer the questions right away, as if this were some sort of checklist. Give yourself some time each day to ponder them, and write down answers whenever and wherever they come to you.

Then go on to the next question, which is about freedom. (And don't say, "Do I *have* to?" I thought of that joke too.)

10

≈≈≈≈

What Do I Think Freedom Means?

Freedom is something we talk about a lot, but all you have to do is look at politics in any era to see that we don't all mean the same thing by the word. In Nazi Germany, the Nazi Party appealed to ordinary Germans by promising them "freedom"—it was one of the Nazis' favorite words.

Most of us today would say that the Nazis did not exemplify freedom. What you think *freedom* means, though, will depend on your assumptions about how the world operates. And you may be a little surprised by the results of this self-examination. Maybe freedom means something different to you from what you thought it meant. Or maybe you'll see for the first time that there's a different meaning of *freedom* that you haven't considered.

At first glance, these questions may not seem to have anything to do with freedom at all. But you'll soon see why you're asking them.

1. Long-Term Goals versus Short-Term Desires

Which do I find more interesting and exciting: my long-term goals for reaching lasting happiness or my short-term desires (like ice cream)? It's easy to get sidetracked by the desires of Level 1 and Level 2. Everyone does it to some extent. But this question is inviting you to ask yourself what you really want. If one of those lower-level desires makes you really enthusiastic in a way that the quest for lasting happiness doesn't, then you know how to answer the question. And that's good information. Once again, no one is going to give you a failing grade.

2. Commitment to Long-Term Goals

Do I keep up the level of excitement and commitment to my long-term goals when I run into difficulties? Am I willing to sacrifice some of my short-term comfort or status for the sake of reaching lasting happiness? Sometimes, as we already know, moving ahead on the road to happiness means giving up temporary advantages. What if you have to quit doing something you really enjoy? What if you have to give up a chance at a higher-paying job? This question tells you where your priorities are, so remember to answer it not with what you think you *ought* to be feeling but with what you actually do feel right now.

3. Roadblocks

What roadblocks get in the way of my quest for long-term happiness? Are there addictions or attitudes that hold me back? Do I have the will power to overcome those addictions and attitudes? Addictions doesn't just mean alcoholism or drugs or something we normally think of as an addiction. If you can't get through the day without playing video games, then you may have a gaming addiction. If you can't pass up the opportunity to make a sarcastic remark, even when you know it will make somebody feel bad, then you may have a sarcasm addiction.

Not all addictions are equally harmful. If you have a strong desire for really good apples, and you need to have the best apples on your table all the time, then that may be an addiction, but if it isn't causing you to neglect the other aspects of your life, it's not a very harmful one. But if something is keeping you from moving ahead with your plans for long-term happiness, that's a harmful addiction.

4. Attitude toward the Sacrifices Required by Commitment

Do I resent it if I have to make sacrifices to be committed to one person or to one important ideal? This gets to the core of our main question about freedom. Let's say you've been married for a while. Marriage is supposed to restrict you to *one* partner for the rest of your life. Does that seem like an assault on your freedom?

Once again, think these questions over for a while. Don't try to answer them all at once. You may come up with different answers after you've been meditating for a few days or even weeks.

What you'll probably be learning is what the idea of "freedom" conveys to you, and it's very likely that it conveys the wrong notion.

By *wrong* I mean that your idea of freedom will stand in your way.

There are two main ways of thinking about freedom:

1. Freedom *from*
2. Freedom *for*

In our Western culture, we tend to think of the first one exclusively, but to move ahead toward lasting happiness, you're going to need to think in terms of the second one.

What does this distinction mean?

If you think mostly in terms of freedom *from*, you see anything that stands in the way of doing *whatever you want* as an assault on your freedom. This is probably the way most Americans think of freedom, but it's a very limiting way of thinking about it. In fact, it ultimately *restricts* your freedom.

Why do I say that? Because everything worth doing over the long term requires a commitment. I used the example of marriage earlier, and that's probably the most obvious one. You can freely choose marriage—but once you have made that commitment, you no longer have freedom to choose not to be married. Yet that commitment is precisely what makes marriage worth choosing. We *want* a permanent relationship. We want to have a family and a place in the world that doesn't depend on our whims. We want to have a stable, secure environment for ourselves and our children. We want to have a relationship where emotional intimacy and self-sacrifice for each other can grow. We want to be able to wake up in the morning and know "I am where I belong." And in order to do that, we need to be able to make a commitment.

The same is true for all sorts of other things. If you want to be able to play in a band, you have to commit to showing up for the rehearsals. That may mean that you're no longer free to do whatever you want on Thursday night—but you get to play in a band. You're having a far better time than you would if you just kept yourself free from all commitments.

That's what we mean by "freedom *for*." When you start thinking of long-term happiness, this is the kind of *positive* freedom you begin to see as important. You want to be free to make a commitment to what you think is worthwhile. If you think exclusively in terms of freedom *from*, you shut yourself out of everything that leads to more profound and even ultimate happiness.

We've spent all this time on these questions because they give us a good idea of where we are on the happiness ladder so far. They also make us think about where we'd like to be and what might be holding us back. Keep thinking about them, and keep writing down your insights whenever they occur to you.

Meanwhile, it's time to start thinking about that last and highest level of happiness—the transcendent. I already admitted that I'm going to have to do some more work to convince you that such a thing even exists. But Levels 3 and 4 are intimately related, and I don't think you'll get far if you try to stop at Level 3. So here we go. Let's get to work.

11

~~~~~

Why Level 4?

We got up to that third level, and life is better. It's not perfect, but it's better. Why wouldn't we stop there?

The answer is that we're not built to stop there. We seem to be built for something more.

Think back to the times when you've been with the people you care about most. I'm going to assume for the moment that you have a family that you love and plenty of good friends — even though I know there are quite a few people in America who don't have those things. Let's assume your life is pretty good by any reasonable standard. Have you ever been at a family gathering, or with some of your closest friends at a party, and suddenly felt all alone in the world?

It's a more common experience than you'd think. In fact, it's so common that I'm betting you've had it at some point. You're at a place where you should feel at home, with the people you should feel most comfortable with, yet you feel as though you don't belong there. Something is wrong. You're not feeling completely at home in this group. You're lonely. You're bored.

If that happens to you, there's nothing wrong with you. You're absolutely normal. Your mind is doing what it was built to do. It's pointing you to the transcendent: the world beyond what you can see and hear and touch, but the world your mind knows it's meant for.

As we saw in chapter 8 (section 9), we have four *transcendental desires* that inspire us toward the fourth level of happiness. We also have five feelings indicating a lack of transcendental fulfillment.

A transcendental desire is for something that cannot exist in the material world but that we seem to be aware of—as if it were present to us or in us.

Let's begin with the feelings that indicate a lack of something on the transcendent level.

Five Feelings Indicating Lack of Transcendental Fulfillment

These feelings tell us that something is missing in our lives that cannot be filled by material things or even human beings. For lack of a better term, I will call the feelings indicating a lack of transcendence *cosmic*, in the sense of "other worldly." Let's look at each of them—cosmic boredom, cosmic emptiness, cosmic alienation, cosmic loneliness, and cosmic guilt.

Cosmic Boredom

Think about boredom for a while. Boredom is a very interesting subject when you put some thought into it. How could we ever be bored? We live in a world where the distractions are infinite. If you have a smartphone—and I have to go a long way to meet someone who doesn't have a smartphone these days—then there's a whole universe of entertainment in your pocket. You could watch a movie on it. You could read a book. You could go on X and get into a lively debate about cooking. There's no need to be bored.

And that's just your phone. Even if you're locked in a room without your phone, you have an endless supply of memories stored up in your own mind that you could replay. You could think over plans for the future. You could imagine a story like *Star Wars*, but better.

We fill our lives with distractions—like our phones, for example—but they eventually bore us. Even when we have everything, a sense of boredom frequently overtakes us. How can this happen in our stimulus-saturated world?

If having everything in my pocket isn't enough, what could possibly satisfy me? How can almost endless stimulation be insufficient to maintain my interest and excitement?

Many existentialist philosophers—both Christian and non-Christian—propose that we are lacking not material and human fulfillment but, rather, transcendental fulfillment. In chapter 8 (section 9), we explored our transcendental desires that are oriented toward ever-greater truth, love, fairness/justice, and beauty. From this we might infer that when we try to obtain transcendental fulfillment—ever-greater truth, love, justice, and beauty—from something that is merely material, that material object or creature cannot help but fail to satisfy us, and so we are overcome by boredom. So it seems that the only solution to persistent boredom is transcendental fulfillment—connection with transcendental truth, love, justice, and beauty—a connection with an ultimate or supreme being. If so, then boredom is the call of the transcendent.

If you have experienced this persistent boredom, try an experiment—open yourself to an ultimate or supreme being who might provide some satisfaction of your desire for transcendent truth, love, justice, and beauty. It may be the cure of your boredom.

Cosmic Emptiness

Has this ever happened to you? You're standing in front of a mirror preparing your hair or shaving, and as you look at yourself, you get a feeling of tremendous emptiness inside you—a deep void, a lack of substance. It can be so intense that you literally have to stop what you're doing and get away from the mirror. Like cosmic boredom, this sense of being virtually nothing indicates that something is missing. While cosmic boredom indicates that something is missing in the material world, cosmic emptiness indicates that something is missing *in us*.

This feeling reveals that we are not and cannot be ultimate meaning for ourselves, the ultimate ground of our identity, or even ultimate fulfillment for ourselves: we are insufficient or incomplete beings in ourselves—radically in need of something that is sufficient, grounded, and meaningful *in itself*. Without this truly ultimate reality, we feel like nothing.

Why would we feel like nothing with all our powers of intellection, creativity, aesthetic sensibility, goodness, and love? Something must exist within us that tells us that our powers are *not* ultimate. Yes, they are truly remarkable powers, but they are not sufficient to be ultimate for meaning, grounding, and fulfillment in our lives—they are not sufficient in themselves. It would not be surprising that this "something" is like Eddington's "light that beckons ahead"—"the something" that incites our transcendental desires for ever-greater truth, love, justice, and beauty.

Cosmic Alienation

Alienation is the feeling that you don't belong, that you're in a foreign place, that you are not at home. You may feel like you are at home when you are with your family or feel like you belong at your job, but right in the midst of these positive feelings, you sense that you are not really at home. You seem to feel that no worldly home can be your real home. Sometimes, it feels like you are out of sorts with the totality—the whole of reality—and the world seems cold and dark.

How can we feel like we're not at home in the whole of reality when we are sitting comfortably at home? Once again, we may infer that there is something missing in our worldly home—something missing in all worldly homes.

What is the origin of this alienation from the world and the whole of reality? It seems to be connected to a sense of what perfect or ultimate home is like. When we try to make our personal home or some other worldly dwelling our perfect home, the sense of perfect home within us rises up, as it were, in protest. Our inner sense is telling us that we will not find ultimate peace and fulfillment through this imperfect home because we are made for something more—something ultimate and unsurpassable.

Is this the call of Eddington's transcendent light within us, revealing what we are *really* meant for and who we *really* are? If so, then the unpleasant feelings of coldness, darkness, and restlessness have a very positive outcome because they are preventing us from under-living our lives, underestimating our dignity, and undervaluing our true nature and destiny. But the alienation does more—it calls us to ultimacy, to transcendence, and to the light that beckons ahead.

Cosmic Loneliness

We already saw how essential love is to our happiness. That was one of the elements that pushed us from Level 2 up to Level 3.

Human love is a wonderful thing, and it goes a long way toward healing the hole in our hearts that we feel when we focus only on our material and comparative desires. But it's not enough. As we saw above, even when we are surrounded by people we love, we can still feel deeply lonely, as if we haven't found the love we were looking for. Try as we might, other human beings seem to always manifest imperfections in sensitivity, understanding, responsiveness, and care—imperfections in love.

The Four Levels of Happiness

It seems that this sense of cosmic loneliness—being alone in the whole of reality—is connected with our desire for ultimate or ever-greater love (discussed in chapter 8), but it works in an inverse way. While driving us to look for more perfect love, this transcendental desire also fills us with cosmic loneliness when we try to find ultimate or perfect love in all the wrong places: human beings, human community, and the material world. Eddington's transcendent light seems to be at once urging us toward perfect love, while preventing us from investing ourselves in imperfect love.

Cosmic Guilt

Guilt is a feeling all humanity knows and experiences. You can probably think of a list of points you feel guilty about right now. But there's even more to it than that list. Even if you checked off all the items on that list—even if you found the driver you cut off in traffic this morning and gave her an apology and an ice-cream cone—you'd still have a feeling of guilt. But why?

We seem to have a sense that there is some kind of residual damage or negative effect that remains in a person we have hurt or offended—even after we have asked for forgiveness and given them an ice-cream cone. Sometimes we also extend this negative effect to the family and friends of the people we have offended, and sometimes we go further. As in the case of Josef K. in Franz Kafka's *The Trial*, we may even feel that our offense has damaged the "cosmos"—the harmonious spiritual unity among us. We feel that the damaging effects of our offensive action have a ripple effect that just keeps flowing outward—and that asking for forgiveness from the offended person can't undo the damage to this harmonious unity.

I was once sitting in a Denver hotel waiting to meet a friend, and a woman sat down next to me. Recognizing that I was a priest by my collar, she said, "I wish I could be like you Catholics, go to

Confession, and be absolved of the damage I've done to others." I was surprised by that introductory line, but I couldn't help myself. I asked, "Do you believe in God? And if so, do you believe that asking for His forgiveness would in some sense undo the damage you've caused by your words and actions?" She replied, "Well, I wish I could believe in God."

After I gave her a summary of evidence from contemporary physics for an intelligent creator and evidence of an afterlife from medical studies of near-death experiences (see chapter 12),[14] she began to get a glimmer of hope. When my friend came, I gave the woman a little prayer for forgiveness: "Lord, please make good come out of whatever harm I might have caused."

I can't tell you the end of this story, but I tell it because it illustrates that we have a sense not only of personal guilt but also of cosmic guilt, and as I said above, we have this guilt even if we are not religious. Most existentialist philosophers—both religious and nonreligious—have recognized this sense of cosmic guilt. The religious existentialists (e.g., Søren Kierkegaard, Martin Buber, Gabriel Marcel, Paul Ricoeur, and Karl Jaspers) ask God for forgiveness and atonement (reparation for their offenses). Atheistic existentialists (e.g., Friedrich Nietzsche, Jean-Paul Sartre, Albert Camus, and Franz Kafka) feel cosmic guilt as much as religious existentialists, but since they have no way of attaining transcendent forgiveness and atonement, they declare the human condition to be absurd and filled with meaningless pain. If these philosophers are a good sample, then cosmic guilt is a reality.

You might ask yourself the question "How could we have a sense of cosmic guilt unless we had some sense of a harmonious

---

[14] See Robert Spitzer, *Science at the Doorstep to God: Science and Reason in Support of God, the Soul, and Life after Death* (San Francisco: Ignatius, 2023), chaps. 4–6.

transcendent/spiritual reality with which we are connected?" If
your answer is something like "I don't think we could," then the
next question is "Where did you get this sense of a harmonious
transcendent/spiritual reality that is involved in your actions?"
From my vantage point, this harmonious transcendent/spiritual
reality seems very similar to Eddington's transcendent light that
beckons ahead—the light that fuels our drive for ever-greater truth,
love, justice, and beauty, as well as our feelings of cosmic boredom,
cosmic emptiness, cosmic alienation, and cosmic loneliness. If
so, then cosmic guilt is yet another call or invitation from the
transcendent light not to underlive our lives, underestimate our
dignity, and undervalue our true nature and destiny. Notice that
this transcendent light is not giving us an irresistible answer and
making the decision for us. Rather, it gives us clues, desires, feelings of transcendence, and negative feelings of its absence. The
choice is ours.

So much within us seems to be pushing us to take a leap of
faith and embrace the transcendent. Yet so much in our world
today seems to be trying to hold us back. Popular culture wants us
to stop at pleasure, the material, and ego-comparative happiness
(Levels 1 and 2). If we seem to have a desire for something more,
that's just because the world is tragically absurd.

So if we're going to take a leap of faith, we're going to have to
be convinced that there really is something on the other side of
that gap. Let's see if we can get even more clarity about the reality
and nature of this transcendent light by a deeper exploration of
our transcendental desires.

The Divine within Our Transcendental Desires

Let's take a new look at the transcendental desires through the
lens of some of the world's greatest philosophers to see what they

reveal through their philosophical reflections. The forthcoming argument is not easy, but it opens upon the heart of some of the greatest ideas ever conceived and proven. I hope you will give it a shot because it shines light on the truth of our nature and even reality itself—the light of some of the greatest minds that ever existed.

The Divine in Our Sense of Perfect Truth

Recall from chapter 8 that we spend a lot of our mental energy on working out what's *true* and distinguishing it from what's *false*. We have the scientific method to keep us from wandering too far off the road to truth, and we have some fairly sophisticated instincts that are meant to protect us from falsehood. Yet the truth always seems to be just beyond us.

Not that we don't have knowledge, and amazing knowledge at that. We can know that certain facts are true beyond any reasonable doubt. Science has made enormous progress in working out the laws by which the universe operates. We can measure huge distances. We can know what will happen when we perform a controlled chemical experiment. We can identify a species of bacterium that we can't even see. These are wonderful things, and they fascinate us.

But we want more. Every scientist would like to be able to answer every question about the physical world correctly; every philosopher would like to answer every metaphysical question about reality correctly; and every one of us wants, at least tacitly, to know everything about everything. Some philosophers call this "the unrestricted desire to know."[15]

---

[15] See, for example, Bernard Lonergan, *Insight: A Study of Human Understanding*, in vol. 3 of *Collected Works of Bernard Lonergan*, ed. Frederick E. Crowe and Robert M. Doran (Toronto: University of Toronto Press, 1992), 245–247 and 372–375.

The Four Levels of Happiness

In chapter 8 and in the previous section, we spoke of Sir Arthur Eddington's intuition that all of us have a transcendent light in us that continuously beckons us beyond our current state of knowledge, provoking us to get to the *whole* truth.

In addition to Eddington, philosophers of science and metaphysics, such as Plato and Aristotle (in the ancient world) and Jacques Maritain, Alfred North Whitehead, and Bernard Lonergan (in the contemporary world), were fascinated by our ability to continuously ask questions—seemingly indefinitely. Somehow, we *always* seem to know that our current state of knowledge is incomplete, which provokes us to ask more questions. This caused the above philosophers to ask, "How can we be continuously aware of the *incompleteness* of our knowledge without being at least tacitly aware of what *complete* knowledge—the whole truth—is like?"

But where could we have gotten this sense of *complete* knowledge —the *whole* truth? We could not have gotten it from the material world, because the truths about our physical world, our universe, and even other possible universes cannot be complete—they still give rise to further questions *beyond* themselves. Hence, they, too, do not embrace the *whole* truth. So, if our sense of the *whole* truth doesn't come from the world around us, or even the universe or multiverses, where did we get our sense of the *whole* truth?

The above philosophers believed that it would have to come from something that is not material or restricted, because material and restricted realities give rise to further questions *beyond* themselves. This means that the source of our awareness of the *whole* truth would have to be an unrestricted, immaterial (spiritual) intelligence. This is the only source that would not give rise to further questions beyond itself.[16]

---

[16] See Lonergan, *Insight*, 657–708.

Notice that since this perfect intelligence is immaterial, it cannot be a *material* (physical) brain but, rather, a reality that is purely spiritual intelligence—and unrestricted as well. Remember, if it is *restricted*, it will give rise to further questions *beyond* itself and therefore would not be *complete* knowledge—the *whole* truth. These philosophers call this unrestricted purely spiritual intelligence "God." Bernard Lonergan provides an extensive proof of this in his comprehensive work *Insight: A Study of Human Understanding.*

If these philosophers are correct, then the unrestricted spiritual intelligence (God) not only exists but is present in our consciousness. Our sense of the *whole* truth (coming from the presence of this perfect intelligence in our consciousness) fuels not only our capacity for ceaseless questioning but also our drive toward ever-expanding creativity.

If this insight is correct, then you may want to ask why an unrestricted perfect spiritual intelligence would want to be present to your consciousness. Why would such a reality do this if it were indifferent to you? If you matter this much, then perhaps this perfect intelligence cares about you.

The Divine in Our Sense of Perfect Love

Has this ever happened to you—or someone you know? You fall in love, appreciating your beloved's uniquely good, lovable, and transcendent qualities, but then begin to see more and more imperfections in them. You begin to think, "They have this annoying habit, and they are not perfectly understanding or perfectly sensitive or perfectly responsive. They are even clueless to my deeper self and fall short in so many different areas. They even grow tired and stressed and get impatient. I guess they're not the one—better to break up and save myself the pain and inconvenience."

The Four Levels of Happiness

What were we looking for? It would seem to be something like perfect love; however, we were trying to find it in imperfect human beings. Since those individuals can't possibly live up to the expectation of being perfectly understanding, authentic, responsive, and untiring in their love, we give up on them and seek another imperfect human being from whom to extract perfect love.

Plato and modern philosophers, such as Gabriel Marcel and Max Scheler, ask a further question: "Why are we always trying to extract perfect love from imperfectly loving human beings? What provokes us to do this?" In chapter 8, we proposed that Eddington's "light that beckons ahead" applies not only to our desire for the whole truth but also to our desire for ever-greater love.

In the context of love, how might we describe the "light that beckons ahead"? The above philosophers reasoned that in addition to being unrestricted and perfect intelligence, "the light" must also be something like perfect love that incites us to measure the people we know against it. We even measure ourselves against it. And so we always seem to be in a state of dissatisfaction about the love of other people and ourselves. We simply don't measure up to the standard of love we're looking for.

How did we get this "light," this sense of perfect love? Where would it have come from? It does not seem like it could come from other people, who are imperfectly loving. Even our mothers are not perfectly loving. So where else could it have come from — and how can it be present in just about everyone, except sociopaths? The above philosophers reasoned that it must come from a cause that is perfectly loving and present in our consciousness. Since it is present in our consciousness, it must be like an idea, rather than a physical substance, and so the cause seems to be immaterial or spiritual — just like the unrestricted spiritual intelligence, which causes our sense of the *whole* truth — what Lonergan calls "God."

Now the conclusion—if the light that causes our sense of perfect love is the same as the unrestricted spiritual intelligence (the cause of our sense of the *whole* truth), then what Lonergan calls "God" is perfectly loving and universally present in human consciousness.

The Divine in Our Sense of Perfect Fairness or Justice

There is another curious fact about human beings. As implied in chapter 8, we have not only a sense of the *whole* truth and perfect love but also a sense of perfect fairness or justice. Have you ever noticed that little children, without really having been taught to do so, can recognize unfairness in just about any inequitable situation? It's not simply times when their sister got more candy than they did, or their brother got a "better" toy at Christmas, but even instances when a parent exemplifies more impatience or strictness toward one sibling over another. Children view unfairness with more importance than just getting the same amount of candy. They *expect* to be treated with perfect fairness, and if they are not, they are likely to have an almost explosive outburst: "That's not fair!" This reveals their sense of betrayal and even the breaking of a solemn trust.

Why the bitter disappointment and feelings of betrayal instead of just saying, "Give me that extra piece of candy"? Why does the issue get blown up so much that it practically takes on cosmic proportions?

It seems that we have not only a sense of what perfect fairness/justice is like but also an expectation that this is what we deserve—and that we *should* not be treated otherwise. As we saw in chapter 8, we even apply this sense of "should" or "ought" to others—we feel like we should not treat others unfairly.

Philosophers have noticed for centuries that this sense of "ought" or "should" does not come from the material world around us. There are "things" out there, but there are no "oughts" out there from which to derive our awareness and expectation of perfect fairness. Additionally, there are no "oughts" out there to incite us to treat others with the same perfect fairness with which we expect others to treat us. So where did we get this "ought" from—this sense that we and others are obligated to be as fair as possible to one another?

In chapter 8, we proposed that Eddington's "light that beckons ahead" applies not only to our sense of the *whole* truth and perfect love but also to our sense of perfect fairness/justice. There is good reason to believe this because, as we saw previously, the cause of our sense of perfect fairness/justice is present in nearly every person, yet beyond the world of material things. If all of us did not get this sense from the world of material things, then we would have to get it from some kind of immaterial (spiritual) reality that can make it interiorly present in almost everyone.

You can probably guess what's coming now. It sounds like the cause of our sense and expectation of perfect fairness is the same as the cause of our sense of perfect love and our sense of the *whole* truth—the unrestricted immaterial (spiritual) perfect intelligence that many philosophers call "God." Thus, it seems that God is not only unrestricted spiritual intelligence but also perfectly loving and perfectly fair/just. This again provokes the question "If this God were indifferent to us—if He did not care about us—why would He even bother to be present in us to incite our sense of perfect truth, love, and fairness/justice?"

The Divine in Our Sense of Perfect Beauty

The next time you look at an advertisement with a model in it, ask yourself, "How did that model get to look so perfect?" I can tell you the answer, which you probably already know yourself: image-editing software.

Why Level 4?

Even the people we consider most beautiful seem to need improvement when we look at them with a critical eye. The same point is true of landscapes that we consider some of the wonders of the world. We have an ideal of beauty in our minds, and the world always fails to meet it. Sometimes it comes close, but we're always dissatisfied. We don't want close. We want perfection.

There is something almost mystical about the beautiful—in nature, great architecture, the human form, art, and music. Though our tastes vary, when we connect with the beautiful, it invariably arouses our passions and makes our hearts soar. The upward motion of the term *soar* shows that it goes *beyond* mere elation or passionate feelings. Good music seems to communicate something transcendent, something ultimately glorious, majestic, joyful—something perfect, like the fit of perfect harmony and melody. Sometimes good music can evoke a kind of ecstasy, a coming out of ourselves. But where do we emerge?

We may here make recourse to Plato—one of the first philosophers to articulate the natural movement from the awareness of beauty to the glory and joy of the "beyond"—the "absolute." In his great work the *Symposium*, Plato speaks of the many kinds of beauty that move us not only to transcendence but to glorious, sublime, and majestic transcendence.[17] He notes that the transcendent is not boring but precisely the opposite—it is the height of spiritual excitement and awakening. This transcendent quality of beauty reveals not only the depth of our aesthetic sensibility but also our natural connection with beauty itself—with divine glory. If Plato and his followers have put their finger on something important, then many of us have a connection with glorious, awe-inspiring transcendence through beauty.

[17] Plato, *Symposium* 210a–211b.

In chapter 8, we proposed that our sense of perfect beauty, and the soaring of our souls toward it, may well be caused by the "light that beckons ahead," which, as we have seen above, is at once perfect intelligence, perfect love, and perfect fairness/justice—an unrestricted, purely spiritual reality (called "God" by many philosophers). If this is correct, then God is not only the source of our unceasing curiosity and creativity but also the source of unceasing excitement, inspiration, and awe.

Conclusion

If any of the above insights are even partially correct, then it is reasonable to conclude that there is an immaterial (spiritual) transcendent reality, which is perfectly intelligent, loving, just, and beautiful, present to our consciousness. If Lonergan and his followers are correct, then this reality is an unrestricted perfect spiritual intelligence—like God. The presence of this spiritual being within our consciousness opens us to an ever more perfect horizon of truth, love, justice, and beauty. Without this spiritual being, God, we would have ceased to seek these transcendental objectives almost immediately and contented ourselves with a comfortable life in a cave eating bananas and coconuts.

If these transcendental considerations reflect the reality of human consciousness, then we all have the Divine Being within us. We radiate His perfection in truth, love, justice, and beauty. And if the Divine Being is present in us, He must care about us—and love us. Given this, we can no longer treat others as mere things or problems; we must treat one another as uniquely good, transcendent mysteries—loved by God. Our happiness depends on it.

12

⋘⋙

Happiness Level 4: There's More to Life Than This

It used to be that everybody believed in a spiritual world, but now we have science, and we "know" that spiritual realities are just superstition.

That's what the world of pop culture tells us. Even religious people fall for this understanding, and it sometimes makes them hostile to science.

That's too bad. Science doesn't eliminate the spiritual. Popular culture has a very unscientific view of science.

But why do we need to think about the world beyond what we see? Didn't we get pretty far with emotional and cognitive empathy? We know that we're more happy when other people are happy, and we know that we should seek to understand other people's situations, not just to feel along with them. That's a better way to happiness than just satisfying our appetites or winning in the comparison game, isn't it?

Well, yes, it is. But it's not enough. As we have seen, we have additional needs, because we're built to desire them.

One of these needs is unconditional love.

As we saw in the previous chapter, we have a built-in need for love. And we also have the freedom to intentionally disappoint people. Christians call that "sin." We may have people who love us dearly, but even they can be disappointed. What we want is to be loved *no matter what*. No human being can ever do that for us because we'll eventually exasperate everybody we know. That doesn't mean they'll stop loving us, but it does mean they won't love us constantly and perfectly the way we want them to. Only someone who is absolutely perfect could do that. Only someone completely without faults could see past the temporary annoyances we create for the people around us and could still love us in the midst of our imperfections. And we don't know anyone as perfect as that.

In the last chapter we presented the arguments of several philosophers indicating that our transcendental desires for perfect truth, love, justice, and beauty were caused by the presence of an unrestricted perfect spiritual intelligence within our consciousness. Beyond this philosophical evidence, is there any scientific evidence for the existence of such a reality?

Let's begin with looking at the popular view of science, and then we can look at what science and scientists really do tell us.

Science and the Transcendent

We'll start right at the beginning. People used to believe that God created the universe, but now we "know" that isn't true. The universe is just a series of random chances, and physical laws determine everything that happens.

That's what popular culture tells us, but that view was actually a lot easier to hold on to *before* contemporary science. If the universe had always been there, more or less the way it is now, then we might think this is the way things are and have always been. We could still ask why things have always been this way, but we wouldn't have a beginning to account for.

Enter the Big Bang. It turns out that all our observations show that the universe did have a beginning. The universe has been expanding for about 13.8 billion years, give or take a few.

How do we know that?

One of the most interesting observations astronomers made in the early twentieth century was that the universe was expanding. In fact, the farther away from us something in the universe is, the faster it is moving away from us. The difference in speed is uniformly predictable, and the equation that describes this phenomenon is known as the Hubble-Lemaître law. It's also known as Hubble's law, but the International Astronomical Union officially added Lemaître's name to acknowledge that he was the first to discover it.[18]

Who was Lemaître? Msgr. Georges Lemaître was a priest in Belgium who first proposed the big bang theory. He realized that the observations astronomers were making with their new equipment in the early twentieth century could only be explained if the universe were expanding, and he worked out the rate of expansion. (The calculations were refined by another astronomer, Edwin Hubble, a few years later, and Hubble's article was much more widely read than Lemaître's.) Everything fits together if we understand that the whole universe expanded from a single point—what Lemaître called the primordial atom.

Some of the world's top scientists resisted the idea for a while —even Albert Einstein was unconvinced at first. But Lemaître did the patient scientific work and showed that the hypothesis accounted for the facts. Einstein was convinced: he was one of the scientists who nominated Lemaître for Belgium's top science award. Everybody else came to the same conclusion. Msgr. Lemaître insisted that theology had nothing to do with his conclusions: he just followed the science. Other scientists followed his science, too, and they ended up in the same place: the universe began at a particular time in the finite past, expanding from a single point.

Once the scientific world had accepted the theory, the popular press had to give it a name. "Big bang" was originally a description of the theory by one of the astronomers who didn't accept it, but the theory stuck and so did the name.

Now, why is this important? Well, if the universe had just been there all the time, we could have avoided the question of how it started. But if it had a beginning, then it began for some reason. Many of the scientists who ultimately accepted the big bang theory would have preferred not to because a steady-state universe — a universe that had always been the way it is, and always would be the way it is — doesn't pose the question of how it all began.

Since the time of Lemaître and Hubble, astronomers and cosmologists have tried to postulate a way in which a beginning could be avoided. They came up with multiverses (hypothetical super-universes that produced huge numbers of bubble universes, one of which is like our own), hypothetical bouncing universes (which expand and contract seemingly indefinitely), and even hypothetical super-universes in the higher dimensional space of string theory.[19] They suggested that even if our universe were

---

[19] For an explanation of these hypothetical models, see Robert Spitzer, *Science at the Doorstep to God: Science and Reason in Support of God, the Soul, and Life after Death* (San Francisco: Ignatius, 2023), chaps. 1–2. See also Robert Spitzer, *New Proofs for the Existence of God:*

only 13.8 billion years old, the hypothetical multiverse, bouncing universe, or higher dimensional string universe could have existed eternally in the past.

These hypotheses soon began to break down. First, Arvind Borde, Alan Guth, and Alexander Vilenkin showed that all universal systems with an expansion rate greater than zero had to have a beginning. Then the problem of Boltzmann brains showed that multiverses had to have a beginning and could not have an infinite number of bubble universes. Then Stephen Hawking, Thomas Hertog, and other physicists showed that any multiverse that could generate our universe would have to have a beginning, could not be infinite, and would likely have a very small number of bubble universes.[20]

These discoveries strongly imply that physical reality (whether it be a multiverse, a higher dimensional string universe, or a bouncing universe) had a beginning, and if there really is a multiverse, it would have a small number of bubble universes, most of which are like our own.[21] This is the best that science can tell us today, and it implies that physical reality was created by a transphysical cause—which is highly intelligent (see below).[22]

Once the universe was created, it operated under physical laws that inevitably formed galaxies of stars and planets, one of which was ours. These physical laws are another important piece

Contributions of Contemporary Physics and Philosophy (Grand Rapids, MI: Eerdmans, 2010), chaps. 1–2.

[20] See Spitzer, *Doorstep to God*, chaps. 1–2.
[21] Ibid.
[22] See ibid. See also Robert Spitzer and James Sinclair, "Fine-Tuning and Indications of Transcendent Intelligence," in *Theism and Atheism: Opposing Arguments in Philosophy*, ed. Joseph Koterski, S.J., and Graham Oppy (New York: Macmillan Reference, 2019), 331–363.

of evidence that there is more to life than the physical. These laws are simple and mathematical. They create enormous complexity, but the laws that create all that complexity are relatively few and are remarkably interrelated.

Think of Albert Einstein's big breakthrough. The equivalence of mass and energy has profound effects on how we understand the universe—and our observations confirm that Einstein was right. Strange and wonderful things happen at large scales, and we've had to revise our whole idea of how time works and what distance means. But much of this enormous complexity arises from the equation $E = mc^2$.

What does it mean that the universe works by simple laws? Einstein himself concluded that these laws were evidence of a *superior mind*. The fact that mathematics can describe our universe so precisely is evidence that there is intelligence behind creation. Einstein was not traditionally religious, but he couldn't help concluding that there was something behind the creation of the rational universe, and that something could best be named God.

"While it is true that scientific truths are entirely independent from religious or moral considerations," Einstein wrote, "those individuals to whom we owe the great creative achievements of science were all of them imbued with the truly religious conviction that this universe of ours is something perfect and susceptible to the rational striving for knowledge."[23] Without this "religious" conviction that the world is rational, science never even begins.

Einstein changed the way we think about things on the very big scale. Max Planck, the father of quantum physics, changed how we think about the very, very small. He believed that religion and

[23] Albert Einstein, *Ideas and Opinions* (New York: Crown, 1995), 52.

science have the same goal: recognizing the all-powerful intelligence that rules the universe. For Planck, the more we understand the universe, the more we should be moved to humble reverence.[24]

Einstein and Planck are probably the two most influential scientific minds of modern times, and both believed that there is a *transcendent reality* — a realm of existence beyond the physical. The fact that we can understand the universe, they thought, shows us that there's an intelligence behind it.

Werner Heisenberg was pretty close to Einstein and Planck in how influential he has been in the scientific world. He was most famous for his "uncertainty principle," which tells us that, for subatomic particles, knowing *one* thing about them means we can't know *another* — for example, we can know the *position* of a particle but not its *momentum*, or vice versa. Heisenberg himself was a lifelong Christian, and he believed that the knowledge denied to our human brains was accessible to God. "Although I am now convinced that scientific truth is unassailable in its own field," he said, "I have never found it possible to dismiss the content of religious thinking as simply part of an outmoded phase in the consciousness of mankind."[25] Like Planck, he believed that religion and science together were both necessary to understand the world.

You'll notice that this is completely opposite the pop-culture view of the opposition of science and religion. Planck and Heisenberg made it explicit: science and religion are two branches of the same effort to understand the world. Science can tell us the empirical-mathematical how of the physical world but not the why, while

[24] See Raymond Seeger, "Planck, Physicist," *Journal of the American Scientific Affiliation* 37, no. 4 (December 1985): 232–233.

[25] Werner Heisenberg, "Erste Gespräche über das Verhältnis von Naturwissenschaft und Religion," in *Religion-Wissenschaft-Weltbild*, ed. Werner Trutwin (Düsseldorf: Patmos Verlag, 1970), 23–31.

religion can tell us the why but not the empirical-mathematical how. When the two complement one another, it gives a satisfying explanation not only of the rational character of the universe but also the character of intelligence itself (see chapter 11).

Fine-Tuning for Life and Transcendent Intelligence

This section may be challenging, but my intent is to give only the *main* idea that scientific evidence shows the strong likelihood of a transcendent intelligence that created our universe in a way that can sustain life. If you can understand the details, that is great. If not, the main idea, when combined with other evidence, is more than enough.

What does "fine-tuning for life" mean? Since 1927 (when Msgr. Lemaître discovered the big bang theory), scientists have identified more than twenty initial conditions and constants of our universe that determine the parameters of our physical laws, processes, and structures. You have probably heard of some of these constants, such as the speed of light constant, Planck's constant, the cosmological constant, the gravitational constant, the mass of the proton, the mass of the electron, and the electromagnetic charge. A very small variation in the numeric values of these constants at the big bang would have led to a completely different universe that would almost certainly have been hostile to life.

Now, here's the fine-tuning problem. These initial constants are not determined by our physical laws, and so they could have had virtually any numeric value within a huge range at the big bang. However, only an exceedingly small range of these constants can give rise to the occurrence, development, and evolution of life-forms. If these constants could have had virtually any number within a huge range at the big bang, but only an exceedingly small range will give rise to life, then the odds of life occurring by pure chance in our universe at the big bang is exceedingly, exceedingly small—virtually impossible.[26] Let's give a few examples that have baffled physicists for at least four decades.

Low Entropy

Our universe has very low entropy. Low entropy means that the universe has a large amount of the order needed for physical change and activity. High entropy would mean very little order required for change and activity. Low entropy would have been fatal for the development of any life-form in our universe. Put simply, we need very low entropy to have a universe capable of giving rise to life-forms and their development.

Now, here is the problem: Famous Oxford physicist Roger Penrose calculated the odds against our universe having this low entropy by pure chance at the big bang. It is one chance in $10^{10^{123}}$. This number is so large that it is about the same odds as a monkey typing the entire corpus of Shakespeare *perfectly* by random tapping of the keys in a *single* try. Evidently, this is virtually impossible. This means that life occurring by pure chance in our spacious universe is virtually impossible.

So how did the universe get such low entropy? We will explain this after giving another example.

The Cosmological Constant

The cosmological constant is the value of the energy density of the vacuum of space. This is a very fancy way of saying the following:

---

[26] See Geraint Lewis and Luke Barnes, *Fortunate Universe: Life in a Finely Tuned Cosmos* (Cambridge: Cambridge University Press, 2016), 1–182. See also Spitzer and Sinclair, "Transcendent Intelligence," 331–363.

The Four Levels of Happiness

If the cosmological constant had an exceedingly tiny variation in its value—higher or lower—at the big bang, then the universe would have either expanded too quickly or contracted into a big crunch. Either option would have been fatal to the development of any life-form in our universe.

Nobel Prize–winning physicist Steven Weinberg showed just how small this constant's possible variation could be. It could only vary by one part in 10^{120}, which is one part in a trillion trillion trillion trillion trillion trillion trillion trillion trillion trillion. That's like attempting to hit a single pinpoint within our entire Milky Way Galaxy in one try—virtually impossible.

There are many other finely tuned constants for life in our universe.[27]

So how could low entropy, the cosmological constant, and other constants have gotten the virtually impossible precise values they needed to have for life to develop in our universe? There are two basic scientific options: a multiverse with about $10^{10^{123}}$ bubble universes in it—or a highly intelligent Creator. The first option—a multiverse with $10^{10^{123}}$ bubble universes—contradicts Stephen Hawking's and Thomas Hertog's discovery that our universe could only have been generated by a multiverse with a *beginning* and *very few* bubble universes, most of which are like our own.[28] It also

---

[27] Some of these are described in Spitzer and Sinclair, "Transcendent Intelligence," 331–341.

[28] Stephen Hawking and Thomas Hertog, "A Smooth Exit from Eternal Inflation?," *Journal of High Energy Physics* (2018), https://doi.org/10.1007/JHEP04(2018)147. See also Andre Pattenden, "Taming the Multiverse: Stephen Hawking's Final Theory about the Big Bang," University of Cambridge Research, May 2, 2018, https://www.cam.ac.uk/research/news/taming-the-multiverse-stephen-hawkings-final-theory-about-the-big-bang.

contradicts the work of other important physicists.[29] This leaves us with only one realistic option from a scientific point of view: a highly intelligent Creator.

Perhaps this evidence is one of the main reasons why most scientists and physicians today profess belief in God (detailed later in this chapter). Sir Fred Hoyle, the father of stellar nucleosynthesis and probably the foremost atheist in the physics community, changed his mind and affirmed his belief in transcendent intelligence when confronted by several inexplicable instances of fine-tuning for life (particularly the occurrence of the carbon atom). He noted in this regard:

> Would you not say to yourself ...: Some super-calculating intellect must have designed the properties of the carbon atom, otherwise the chance of my finding such an atom through the blind forces of nature would be utterly minuscule.... A commonsense interpretation of the facts suggests that a superintellect has monkeyed with physics, as well as with chemistry and biology, and that there are no blind forces worth speaking about in nature. The numbers one calculates from the facts seem to me so overwhelming as to put this conclusion almost beyond question.[30]

Can There Be Science without Belief?

Think back to your high school geometry class. (We're not actually going to do any geometry here, so don't worry—you don't have

[29] See, for example, Tom Banks, "Why I Don't Believe in Eternal Inflation," Preposterous Universe, October 24, 2011, https://www.preposterousuniverse.com/blog/2011/10/24/guest-post-tom-banks-contra-eternal-inflation-2/.

[30] Fred Hoyle, "The Universe: Past and Present Reflections," in *Engineering and Science* (Pasadena, CA: California Institute of Technology, 1981), 12.

to skip this paragraph.) Geometry is all about proving statements about the nature of angles and polygons and circles. Every step of the way, you have to be rigorously logical and show that your conclusion follows inevitably from what's already been established. But at the beginning, there are no proofs. All of geometry starts with *axioms*—things that are true but can't be proved. You have to accept the axioms, even though no one can prove that they're true, or geometry doesn't happen. The entire science of geometry is based on *belief*—intellectual faith.

All sciences are like that. We accept as an *axiom* the idea that the universe is rational. Though there is considerable evidence for its rationality, we still have to *assume* that the same causes will always produce the same effects. Those same causes don't produce one effect on Tuesday and a completely different effect on Thursday. If they did, we could never have any science at all. Even beginning to study the world scientifically requires *belief* (intellectual faith) that the world can be studied scientifically. This faith is outside science: it comes before science can happen.

That in itself is a good reason for a scientist to believe in something beyond the physical. Hence, science and mathematics show us that there has to be something beyond science because science can never include all the necessary ingredients for knowledge.

Kurt Gödel was born in what is now the Czech Republic, although in 1906 it was part of the Austro-Hungarian Empire. He was still in his twenties when he published his incompleteness theorems, which changed the way we thought of mathematics. Of all the sciences, mathematics seems as though it ought to be the most precise and sure-footed, the one that leaves nothing uncertain. Yet Gödel showed that, if a system of mathematics does not contradict itself, it cannot be complete—meaning that it can't prove or disprove some statements in that system. The system also can't prove its own consistency.

What this means is that mathematics itself needs something outside mathematics to make sense. Even the science of numbers requires transcendence—an input from the world outside of science.

Gödel, whose discoveries changed the history of logic, believed that an afterlife was a logically provable thesis. It was a necessary consequence from the fact that the universe is rational.

As can be seen from the above, many of the foremost scientific minds in history—such as Einstein, Planck, Heisenberg, Eddington, Gödel, and many others—all believed in a transcendent world. We should also remember Msgr. Lemaître, the Catholic priest whose discovery of the primordial atom made our modern understanding of the universe possible.

By the way, there's a funny coda to the story of Msgr. Lemaître and the big bang theory. In 2019, a pro-science organization calling itself CivicScience did a survey to find out how much Americans' prejudices affect their opinions of science. The survey asked the question "Should schools in America teach the creation theory of Catholic priest Georges Lemaître as part of their science curriculum?" Only 20 percent of respondents said yes. In the same survey, only 29 percent answered yes to "Should schools in America teach Arabic numerals as part of their curriculum?" Arabic numerals are the numerals 1, 2, 3, 4, and so on, as opposed to the Roman numerals I, II, III, IV, and so forth. This survey tells us that Americans' opinions about science frequently have more to do with prejudice than with real scientific knowledge, which is useful to remember when we're evaluating what popular culture tells us about science and the transcendent.

It's also interesting to point out that, when the head of the company that put out the survey took to Twitter to announce his results, he wrote one tweet about the Arabic-numerals question and another about "the creation theory of Catholic priest

Georges Lemaître." By the time the fact-checking website Snopes reported on the survey, the tweet about the Arabic numerals had been shared more than twenty thousand times. The tweet about Msgr. Lemaître had been shared fewer than ten times. It seems that Georges Lemaître has been mostly wiped clean from popular memory. But it is worth remembering that the man who first formed the theory that, so far, best fits the evidence about how the universe began was a Catholic priest as well as an astronomer and physicist.

But Are You Sure?

I know right away that I'm not going to prove beyond a shadow of a doubt that there's a world beyond the material. If I could do that, all debates would end, and I would just have to count my Nobel Prize money and figure out which charities deserve it most.

But what I've tried to do is show you that you ought to take the transcendent seriously because there is considerable scientific and rational evidence for the existence of a highly intelligent creative power behind our life-permitting universe. This creative power may well be an unrestricted spiritual intelligence that is perfectly loving, just, and beautiful, and may also be present to our consciousness. At the very least, the idea that there's more to the universe than the material is something that's worthy of your consideration. You should think about it.

In our popular culture of today, that's hard. Popular culture tells us that science opposes the transcendent. To be a scientist, you have to be an atheist. To be religious, you have to abandon science.

I think I've shown that this is backwards, but the tragedy is that even many Christians accept that dichotomy between religion and science. In America, it may be *most* Christians. They remain Christian because they grew up Christian, or because they have a gut feeling that their faith is true, but they think they have to give up on science and reason to keep their faith.

I repeat: this is backwards. The more you know about science — the more you explore the depths of what science has revealed to us — the more you realize that there is more to the universe than the things we can see and measure.

In fact, it appears that, if anything, the scientific community is trending more *toward* belief in a higher power than away from it. A Pew Research survey found that just over half of scientists believed in God or a higher power — a slight *majority*, and among younger scientists, the number jumped to 66 percent who professed belief in God or a higher power — a two-thirds majority.[31] Furthermore, 76 percent of physicians professed belief in God or a higher power — two-thirds of them declaring that they practice their religion.[32]

Scientific and Medical Evidence for Life after Death

Now let's talk about life after death. This is one of the points that make us nervous in our intellectual culture today. Isn't life after death just naïve wishful thinking?

No. There's good evidence that we should take seriously. Again, I know I'm not going to convince everyone in one chapter, but I think you won't be able to dismiss the idea of life after death by the time I'm finished. You'll understand why intelligent people believe in it — and even why science has converted some of those intelligent people into believers.

---

[31] "Scientists and Belief," Pew Research Center, November 5, 2009, https://www.pewresearch.org/religion/2009/11/05/scientists -and-belief/.

[32] Kristin Robinson et al., "Religious and Spiritual Beliefs of Physicians," *Journal of Religion and Health* 56 (2017): 205–225, https://doi.org/10.1007/s10943-016-0233-8.

The Four Levels of Happiness

First of all, step back for a moment and look at the human species as a whole. We speak thousands of languages. We live on every continent (except, arguably, Antarctica). We have covered the earth and diversified into an endless rainbow of cultures, all with wildly different traditions and beliefs.

But every human culture has believed in life after death. It is not a Western European idea, or a Nigerian idea, or an Indonesian idea, or a Central American idea. It is universal.

At the very least, the universality of the idea means that it has to have developed early in the human species—before we spread out to every habitable place on earth.

Or—this is the other possibility—it's universal because it's true.

It's a universal idea that things fall down when you drop them. It's a universal idea that the sun rises in the east and sets in the west. These are universal ideas because they're true for everybody. They don't change from one culture to another. There are certainly changes in the details: one culture might see the sun as a god driving a fiery chariot across the sky, and another as a dung beetle rolling a ball of flaming dung through the heavens, and yet another as the earth rotating on its own axis and orbiting around the sun. But these changes in details don't change the fundamental fact that the sun appears to be moving from east to west.

When we look at the idea of life after death, we certainly see differences in the detail. However, the idea that the human person lives forever is consistent across cultures on opposite sides of the planet.

Now, you could say that this indicates that humans are stupid and deluded. But it is a fact of anthropology that has to be accounted for somehow.

Yes, but what about science? Doesn't science prove that there's no such thing as life after death?

Certainly not. Science would have a hard time proving a negative proposition like that. But in fact science gives us some good evidence that life really does persist after death. The consistency and frequency of the experiences of people who have actually been clinically dead, and then revived by modern medicine, at least show us that it's *reasonable* to believe in life after death. So, what is this evidence?

Near-Death Experiences

Our current medical technology has reached the point that we can actually revive the dead—under limited circumstances and depending on what you mean by *dead*. We can bring people back whose hearts have completely stopped beating, who have no electrical activity in their brain (marked by a flat EEG, fixed and dilated pupils, and absence of gag reflex). These people would have been permanently dead without modern medical intervention.

The peer-reviewed medical studies of this phenomenon are so extensive that the New York Academy of Sciences indicated in their 2022 proceedings that there is a credible possibility of our consciousness surviving bodily death.[33] There are several previous peer-reviewed medical studies that strongly support the conclusion

[33] See Samuel Parnia et al., "Guidelines and Standards for the Study of Death and Recalled Experiences of Death—a Multidisciplinary Consensus Statement and Proposed Future Directions," *Annals of the New York Academy of Sciences* 1511, no. 1 (May 2022): 5–21, https://doi.org/10.1111/nyas.14740. See also Emily Henderson, "Researchers Publish Consensus Statement for the Study of Recalled Experiences Surrounding Death," News-Medical Life Sciences, April 13, 2022, https://www.news-medical.net/news/20220413/Researchers-publish-consensus-statement-for-the-study-of-recalled-experiences-surrounding-death.aspx.

of the likelihood of consciousness after clinical death, such as Dr. Samuel Parnia and twenty-nine specialists' 2014 study of 2,060 patients at the University of South Hampton Medical School published in the peer-reviewed *Journal of Resuscitation*,[34] Dr. Pim van Lommel et al.'s 2001 study of near-death experiences of 344 patients in the Netherlands published in Britain's most prestigious medical journal, *The Lancet*,[35] and Dr. Bruce Greyson et al.'s multiple studies of near-death experiences at the University of Virginia Medical School's Department of Perceptual Studies.

There are many reasons why these researchers have such strong conviction about the survival of consciousness after clinical death. Three that are grounded in excellent studies are:

1. Verified reports of perfectly accurate observations by patients during the time of their clinical death outside the operating room and even outside the hospital. For example, one lady identified a tennis shoe with a worn left toe on the third floor ledge of the hospital. She was able to see it because she was hovering outside the hospital's third floor looking at it.[36] See, for example, Dr. Janice Holden's analysis of veridical evidence in

[34] Samuel Parnia et al., "AWARE—Awareness during Resuscitation—A Prospective Study," *Journal of Resuscitation* 85, no. 12 (December 2014), https://doi.org/10.1016/j.resuscitation.2014.09.004.

[35] Pim van Lommel et al., "Near-Death Experience in Survivors of Cardiac Arrest: A Prospective Study in the Netherlands," *The Lancet* 358, no. 9298 (December 15, 2001): 2039–2045, https://doi.org/10.1016/S0140-6736(01)07100-8.

[36] Kimberly Clark, "Clinical Interventions with Near-Death Experiences," in *The Near-Death Experience: Problems, Prospects, Perspectives*, ed. B. Greyson and C. P. Flynn (Springfield, IL: Charles C. Thomas, 1984).

near-death experiences from thirty-nine independent studies representing hundreds of cases.[37]

2. Eighty percent of blind people, most of whom were blind from birth, saw for the first time when they were clinically dead (flat EEG, fixed and dilated pupils, etc.). Many of these patients reported perfectly accurate observations of events outside the operating room and hospital.[38] See below the case of Bradley Burroughs.

3. Many patients who moved from this world to a "heavenly domain" encountered deceased relatives who told them of people and incidents that happened long before they were born. These previously unknown facts were verified by researchers at the University of Virginia Medical School.[39]

The case of sixteen-year-old Bradley Burroughs illustrates perfectly accurate observation of a person blind from birth during the time of his clinical death. This patient moved through the operating room and above the hospital and found himself outside in the snow. He gave an accurate description of the tram tracks and the

---

[37] Janice Holden, *Handbook of Near-Death Experiences: Thirty Years of Investigation* (Connecticut: Praeger Press, 2009).

[38] See Kenneth Ring and E. Valarino, *Lessons from the Light: What We Can Learn from the Near-Death Experience* (New York: Insight Books, 2006), chaps. 1–3.

[39] See, for example, Bruce Greyson, "Seeing Dead People Not Known to Have Died: 'Peak in Darien' Experiences," American Anthropological Association, November 21, 2010, http://onlinelibrary. wiley.com/doi/10.1111/j.1548-1409.2010.01064.x/abstract. See also Emily Kelly, B. Greyson, and I. Stevenson, "Can Experiences Near Death Furnish Evidence of Life after Death?," *Omega: Journal of Death and Dying* 40, no. 4 (2000): 513–519, https://doi. org/10.2190/KNTM-6R07-LTVT-MC6K.

snow, and a moving tram (with a sign indicating the direction of the tram on the back) passing by the hospital at the exact moment of his clinical death.[40]

As can be seen, there is considerable evidence supporting the survival of consciousness after clinical death, which has been validated by excellent peer-reviewed medical studies under close scientific scrutiny. At the moment of clinical death, a soul-body (capable of seeing, hearing, thinking, remembering, self-consciousness, and even movement through walls — going outside and above the hospital) leaves the physical body and accurately reports what is going on. In a large number of cases, this soul-body moves beyond this world to a different domain, frequently described as "heavenly." We will examine this below.

Surprisingly, near-death experiences are consistent much of the time. When children have these experiences, they are similar to those of the majority of adults.

The man who came up with the term *near-death experience* was a psychiatrist named Dr. Raymond Moody, who studied more than a thousand examples of near-death experiences. What he found was a surprising consistency. The experiences tended to have certain elements:

1. Time didn't matter. The people having the experience might be in cardiac arrest for only a few seconds, but there was plenty of time for a series of events.

2. The "dead" people often saw their own bodies from an outside perspective, and many of them were able to describe details of the medical procedures that brought them back to life.

---

[40] Lynn Love, "Blind Man Near Death Experience," YouTube video, March 9, 2013, https://youtu.be/YA8L9W7KiOo.

3. Most of these people experienced a kind of review of their lives up to that point.

4. There was a benevolent being—Christians often identified it as Christ, Jews as an angel or God—who was with them for the review and had one question for them: How well had they learned to love?

5. Often relatives who had died appeared in the after-life environment.

6. The people having these experiences were often reluctant to leave what they described as a beautiful place but either decided to go back for the sake of their families or were told it was not yet their time.

The "benevolent being" (see no. 4 above), or what others call "the loving white light," "God," "Christ," or an "angel," was a major part of many peoples' experience. Without exception, they viewed the light as perfect love for them and others. A typical example is that of Linda Stewart, who noted:

> I felt peaceful and loved immeasurably. I knew I was in the arms of a being who cherished me with perfect love and carried me from the dark void into a new reality.... With the eyes of my soul body, I looked to see what held me in such love and I beheld a radiant, Spirit being, so magnificent and full of love that I knew I would never again feel the sense of loss.[41]

These experiences were life-changing. Most of the people who had them came back to life with a different sense of priorities—a sense that making money and getting ahead weren't as important

[41] Kevin Williams, *Nothing Better than Death* (Bloomington, IN: Xlibris Corp, 2002).

as learning how to love the people around them. In almost all cases, the life changes were positive.[42]

But are these just hallucinations? After all, people near death are in a state in which their brains might be under a lot of stress. When people put their brains under stress with certain drugs, for example, the result can be strange hallucinations—seeing things that aren't there—because the normal functioning of the brain has been impaired, and they can't sort out what's real from what's not.

Actually, scientists even before Dr. Moody had been asking exactly those questions. It turns out that the near-death experiences were quite different from ordinary hallucinations.

People who are hallucinating tend to be delusional—they believe things about the world that are demonstrably false. The hallucinations also tend to be conditioned by what those people already believe or desire. The more they use drugs, the more they hallucinate.

Near-death experiences, on the other hand, are strangely consistent. The people having them know exactly what's going on in the world that the rest of us can perceive. The experiences don't seem to depend on what people believed beforehand, and the experiences are more common and more definite when *fewer* drugs are used.[43]

In sum, near-death experiences differ from hallucinations and other materialist explanations in three major respects:

1. Most near-death experiences report observable data 100 percent accurately, but hallucinations are notoriously inaccurate or completely false.

---

[42] Dr. Jeffrey Mishlove, "Life after Life: Understanding Near-Death Experience with Raymond Moody, MD," https://www.intuition-network.org/txt/moody.htm.

[43] John J. Heaney, "Recent Studies of Near-Death Experiences," *Journal of Religion and Health* 22, no. 2 (Summer 1983): 116-130.

2. In all near-death experiences, there is virtually no electrical activity in the brain (flat EEG), but in hallucinations, there must be electrical activity in the brain (because without electrical activity, the brain cannot do anything, including hallucinating).

3. Most near-death experiences are peaceful and inspiring, but hallucinations often provoke anxiety, agitation, and interior disturbance.

The most reasonable conclusion is that these near-death experiences are not hallucinations but the occurrence of consciousness, thought, vision, and movement beyond (and independent of) the physical body.

Though this preponderance of evidence for survival of consciousness after clinical death is significant, it does not meet the standards for a formal scientific proof of life after death, because science is based on experiments on the physical world, but the soul-body that survives clinical death is beyond physical processes and structures. Hence, science is reliant upon indirect evidence such as the reports of verifiable data from clinically dead individuals outside the operating room and hospital as well as most clinically dead blind people. In view of the consensus statement from the New York Academy of Sciences, there is no shortage of scientists who believe this evidence to be reasonable, probative, and responsible.

Dr. Moody himself was convinced by what he found in his studies. He was a firm believer in life after death. "As a matter of fact," he told his interviewer, "I must confess to you in all honesty, I have absolutely no doubt, on the basis of what my patients have told me, that they did get a glimpse of the beyond."[44]

---

[44] Mishlove, "Life After Life."

The Four Levels of Happiness

All this shows us that science isn't against the idea of the transcendent. In fact, there is considerable evidence of intelligent transcendence revealed by science, and as we have seen, the whole enterprise of science depends on axioms from outside the material world. We have to believe at least in the principles of reason and consistency in order for science to work at all, and those beliefs do not come from science.

Because of that, we've seen that most of the scientists whose work shapes the way we understand the world today were believers. They were not all Christians—although a good number of them were. But most believed that there was something beyond the material, and they believed it because they *understood* science, not *in spite of* science. As we have seen, life after death is a reasonable belief for someone with a scientific mind. It's not just a superstition or wishful thinking.

With these points in mind, I think we can confidently say that belief in the transcendent is *reasonable*. I haven't proved to you beyond all possible doubt that there's more to life than this material existence. But I think any reasonable person would say, looking at the evidence, that you have to take the idea seriously. You can't just wave it away and say only superstitious fools believe that stuff.

And that is where the story ends, unless *you* decide to move forward.

Because the next step is going to require faith, you will have to decide that you will trust in a transcendent reality if you want to get to the next level of happiness—which is the only way you can satisfy those four transcendental desires and plug those five gaping cosmic holes. The next step is faith. "I believe so that I may understand," said the ancient Christian thinker Tertullian.

What Freedom Means to God

But here you may have one more question, and it's a good one. If these transcendent desires are God calling us to change our lives, then why doesn't God just change them for us? He's omnipotent, right? That means He can do anything He wants. So if He wants us to be a certain way, why doesn't He just make us that way?

The answer probably won't satisfy you at first: because God values your freedom. God values your freedom so much that He'll let you choose unhappiness rather than force you to make the right decisions.

Well, that stinks. Why doesn't God just sort everything out if He wants us to be happy?

Think about it though: God wants you to love Him and everyone else. But you can't love unless you have the possibility of not loving. Without a choice not to love, your love does not originate from you. If you can only do one thing — i.e., love — then you are programmed to do loving behaviors. Your love is not your own — it comes from the "Programmer."

Furthermore, God wants you to choose what you believe will make you happy, because He does not want to force you to be happy in the way He chooses. If you were compelled to be happy in the way a supernatural force chooses for you, do you think you would really be happy? All we need to do is observe the reaction of children who refuse to follow what parents believe will make them truly happy.

This is why human love is so difficult, but so precious when it does happen. The object of your love has the choice of not loving you. When that person does love you, it feels like a miracle.

God wants your love, but only as your free choice. You can make that choice right now.

The French philosopher Blaise Pascal had a famous analogy. Think of it as a bet — and then look how the odds are stacked in your favor.

You can decide to have faith in a future life, or you can decide to believe that the material world is all there is. Suppose you make

The Four Levels of Happiness

the choice to believe in Heaven. While you're alive on earth, it makes your life better in every way (see the many studies correlating religion with significantly increased happiness in this life—in chapter 17, footnote 52). Then when you die, if you were right, you go to Heaven and live in eternal happiness. If you were wrong, you just die—but the life you had was better because of the choice you made. On the other hand, if you choose not to believe, your life is worse now. Then, when you die, either you miss out on Heaven, or you were right and you just die, but you missed out on all the good things you could have enjoyed while you were alive.

Pascal's Wager is in front of you right now. Which will you choose? Will you go on to the highest level of happiness?

13

~~~

The Leap of Faith

So if we take that leap of faith, what happens? What does it mean to take a leap of faith? Does it mean I just say, "I believe," and then everything falls into place? Unfortunately, it doesn't. "Faith apart from works is dead," as a wise man once said. You have to do some work. But you knew that when you started: There's not a magic happiness pill. No royal road to happiness. You have to earn it.

So what does this leap of faith look like then?

A Conscious Decision

Making the leap of faith that brings you to the fourth level is making a conscious decision. "From now on," you say, "I will see the world differently. I'll look at everything with an eye on the transcendent. I'm going to make that transcendent view of the world my priority. And even if I'm not completely convinced, I'm going to act as if I am."

It wouldn't be faith, after all, if we could see and feel it. I don't have to have faith that there's a chair under me when I'm sitting at my desk. I know there is. I have enough evidence to be sure of it. But I do have to have faith that my ride will come to pick me up at ten o'clock. I can't see that, because it's only 9:42, and the car isn't here yet. But if I don't have that faith, I can't make any plans, and I'll never get to do the things I was going to do today.

It's the same way with your new transcendent view of the world. You may not be able to see the transcendent; your bodily senses don't send you the message that it's there, the way they do with a chair or a car. As we saw before, your mind has been sending you messages about the transcendent all your life, but you may have been ignoring or dismissing them. Now you have to act as though you believe what your mind has been trying to tell you. You have to have faith.

That's what I'm talking about. We wouldn't need faith if the transcendent God were as obvious as the chair or the car, but if we limited ourselves to the material world, we would never make plans for a bigger and better future. What I'm asking you to do is make bigger and better plans for the future, which will take a bigger and better faith than you may have been using so far. But it's the same *kind* of thing. You already know how to do it. You plan something for the future, and you go ahead as if you know it's going to happen. You have to do things and not just think them. You need to act *as if* you believe.

You Need Two Things

What would you do differently if you did believe? You would attend some house of worship, and you would pray.

If you take those two actions, you're likely to succeed. If you don't, you're likely to fail.

Why is that?

Remember why we're here—why we're taking that next step up to the fourth level of happiness. There are things we're designed to want, and we can't have them unless we have a personal relationship with the transcendent. We need to get to know God personally. That relationship is crucial.

This is going to be hard for people who have been conditioned to think in terms of the merely material. Even in our human relationships, we too often value the relationship according to what we're getting out of it right now. Not getting what we want from a partner? It's time to move on.

Now I'm asking you to enter a relationship with someone you can't even see. What would make you do that?

Just as with human relationships, faith now pays off.

God *wants* to reveal Himself to us, but He won't force the revelation on us. We have to be willing to accept that revelation. And just as with human relationships, one of the ways we build the relationship is by listening when the other is talking.

In this case, we have to be open to God's revelation of Himself through other people and through teaching.

First, let's talk about the church community. "No man is an island," said John Donne, and he was onto something. There's a relationship between you and every other human being.

We already discovered at the third level that our happiness depends on other people. We're happy when others are happy.

The church community is, first of all, a place where there are others. In our fragmented world, we forget how valuable that is. The people in any given congregation may not all agree with you politically, or even religiously. In fact, if you go looking for a congregation where everyone agrees with you, you're doing it wrong. But one point you can be sure of is that they're all after the same thing you're after. They all want that higher level of happiness that comes only when we acknowledge the transcendent. They're all human, so some of them will be hard to get along with—although, if you're not used to going to church, you might be amazed by how easy it is to make friends there. But they all want to reach that level of happiness you've decided you want. You'll probably meet people like you—people who are trying to make a change in their lives. You'll watch some of them fail, and that will be discouraging. But you'll see more of them succeed, and that will be inspiring.

You'll begin to realize that this interrelatedness is part of what God created us for. You'll start to understand what Donne meant: we really can't exist alone, no matter how much we think we can.

Why are there so many different religions, then? They're all mutually contradictory, aren't they? If one is right, all the others are wrong, and we're likely to pick the wrong one. So why should we believe in any of them?

Now, I could tell you right now which one is the right one, and you would say, "Yeah, of course you'd say that, because that's the one that pays your bills."

That's a reasonable response.

So I'm going to tell you this: I think you should consider the Catholic Church. But any faith community is better than none, as long as it's not actively evil. I don't think you should join a terrorist cell or a crazy cult. How do you tell which communities are evil? Here's a good clue: The ones that are good bring you closer to your family, the people you love, and even to strangers. The ones that are bad separate you from others. As long as it isn't one of those, I think it's good that you're joining a faith community. I still hope you'll work your way up to the Catholic Church, but you've already made a big step in the right direction.

While it's true that different religions are different, they are similar in many of the important elements. I have to be careful here not to give you the wrong impression. I don't want you to think all religions are equivalent. They're not. I don't want you to think they all teach the whole truth. They don't. But they do all seek the transcendent. They do all teach you that we are all interconnected—that we are all sisters and brothers, as most of them would say. They teach you that you need to be open to that divine principle that has been calling you all your life, and that you're finally beginning to acknowledge with your leap of faith. And they actively work to accomplish what you're trying to accomplish.[45]

How do they do that?

First, they worship God, under whatever name they use. *Worship* means building a relationship with the Divine. I don't think we understand that enough these days. People who don't go to church often think worship is a bunch of meaningless, empty rituals. They have it completely backwards. There are rituals, yes, even in churches that claim to be against "ritual" in religion. But they're not meaningless. Ritual is the way we convey meaning.

Think for a moment about your daily life. It's full of rituals that convey meaning precisely because they're rituals. From the moment you say "Good morning" to the time you say "Good night," you do certain things that aren't *necessary* in the sense of putting food in your mouth or keeping you from getting eaten by a tiger, but they make your relationships with other people work.

This is what the rituals in religious worship do—except that here, because the transcendent is the most important level of our being, the rituals are also more important. Rituals keep us in touch with the Divine and make our relationship with God work. The church we join brings us closer to the personal God.

So these are the reasons you should join some sort of faith community: you build up your relationship with God, you learn more about what it means to embrace the divine part of your life,

[45] These points are evident in Friedrich Heiler's seven common characteristics of major world religions. See Friedrich Heiler, "The History of Religions as a Preparation for the Cooperation of Religions," in *The History of Religions*, ed. Mircea Eliade and J. Kitagawa (Chicago: Chicago University Press, 1959).

and you grow your relationships with other human beings. All these elements make you happier.

There's one more thing about joining a faith community. It's a commitment. That may scare you at first because our Level 1 and Level 2 minds think of commitment as a bad thing. Commitment is the reason we can't do what we want on Sunday morning, right?

But your Level 3 and Level 4 self has to start thinking of commitment as a powerful aid to happiness. Commitment is the reason you *can* do what you want on Sunday morning—because what you really want to do requires more than casual involvement. Everything worthwhile is going to require commitment.

Becoming Like God

But why do we worship in community? Isn't it enough to know that God is there, that He loves us, and that we're grateful to Him?

Those points make a good start.

But God wants more for us than that. God wants us to be *like God*.

This is a little bit hard for people who didn't grow up in a religious tradition to understand. One of the reasons people rebel against God is because they think God wants to boss them around. They think God is a tyrannical despot who enforces arbitrary rules just to keep us in our place. Now, if God is all-powerful, there's nothing they can do about that. So the only way to rebel is to convince themselves that there is no God. Then their mistaken belief in the tyrannical God is just a myth.

They're half-right. The tyrannical-despot part is mythical. What God wants is not to keep us in our place but to lift us up to His place.

It's a little easier to swallow if you think about it in terms of the human relationships you know. Parents set rules for their children, and teachers set rules in the classroom. But if you're a mother, you're not hoping your son will grow up to be your slave for the rest of his life. You're hoping your son will grow up to be a competent, independent adult. The reason you set rules is because you want your son ultimately to be like you—someone who lives adult life on his own and knows how to do it without falling on his face.

The same is true of teachers. They set rules to make the classroom function smoothly. Some of them are better at it than others, and you can probably think of some teachers you remember who seemed arbitrary and tyrannical. Even the best ones aren't perfect. But their ultimate goal is not to have you sitting in that desk in seventh-grade math class for the rest of your life. Their ultimate goal is for you to be functioning adults. In other words, they want you to be like them.

This brings us back to the question we started with: Why do we worship in community? Why am I telling you that you should join a faith community, rather than just work out your happiness on your own? I think Americans are especially susceptible to this idea of finding our own path to the transcendent. We're Americans. Independence is one of our most sacred traditions. We're a nation of individualists, and we don't like people telling us what to do. Remember what we did to old King George when he tried to boss us around! Now you're telling us we should let a church be the boss of us. Why would we like a pope any better than George III?

From the point of view of making us happier, there are plenty of reasons why we would want to learn from and adhere to principles or rules given by a church. Let's begin with the rule to attend public worship regularly.

Church is a place where we're constantly reminded that there's more to life than *this*. Just by showing up to services, we are acknowledging the transcendent. We're devoting part of our life, even if it's only an hour on Sunday morning, to that highest level of happiness.

Many people go beyond that. I became a priest, which is going a little further than Sunday mornings. But millions of Catholics in ordinary secular life go to Mass every day. They don't have to. Even the Catholic Church herself says it's enough to go on Sundays and holy days of obligation. So the people who go to Mass every day are there because they *want* to be there.

Once you get started down the spiritual route, you may find it fascinating—almost addictive, but in a good way. You might find you want to experience more and more, learn more and more.

That was what happened to me. The more I learned, the more I wanted to learn. The more time I spent in the world of the Church, the more time I wanted to spend in it. The Bible was endlessly fascinating to me. I couldn't get enough of Christian art, literature, and music—some of the towering works of the human spirit. I bet you'll have the same experience with your own faith tradition.

In the next few chapters I will try to describe the inspiration and relationship with God and others that come from church participation—benefits that lift us out of Level 1 and Level 2 happiness to our true contributive and transcendent identity. Then, in chapter 17, I will talk about the transformation of our hearts coming from the principles and rules of religion.

14

❦

Inspiration

Have you ever had a really good idea, only to find out later that it was actually a really bad idea? Yes, of course you have because it happens to all of us. But some bad ideas are more disastrous than others.

First of all, even before we go into the spiritual realm, let's remember that a lot of factors can influence our state of mind and emotions. What you had for breakfast can affect how you think about something. Try reading the most inspirational and uplifting book you can think of while you're suffering from indigestion: I guarantee the experience won't be ideal. If you're feeling annoyed about something unrelated, your annoyance can leak into your decisions about everything else. You have to be honest with yourself, and you have to be observant of your own mental states, which isn't always easy.

But even if your digestion is fine and the world has been treating you well today, you may still be pulled in the wrong direction by what most of the world calls evil.

Judaism, Christianity, and Islam, among other religions, believe in a cosmic struggle between spiritual good and spiritual evil. This even goes for Satanists—only they take evil's side. We seem to have a cosmic "myth" built into our unconscious mind (the term *myth* here does not mean "falsity" but rather a primordial explanatory story[46]).

This myth is so powerful it affects not only our dreams but also our sense of higher purpose in life, our feelings, our activities, and our relationships with others. It shows up in the classics of world religions and culture and even in contemporary literature and film in J. R. R. Tolkien's *Lord of the Rings*, J. K. Rowling's *Harry Potter*, and George Lucas's *Star Wars*. The reason these stories are at the top of all-time literary and film sales is that they resonate with the deepest dimensions of our psyches—almost as if the myth and its symbols were present to the psyche itself before we had any capacity to learn about them. Carl Jung studied the presence of these archetypal symbols in the unconscious psyche of children as revealed by their dreams.[47]

In sum, the idea of a real cosmic struggle between good and evil seems to be omnipresent—in our unconscious minds, our world religions, and our literary culture. In the cosmic struggle, good is pitted against evil, and evil is trying to gain the advantage.

You may not believe in evil spirits, but I would say look around you, and you'll see their work everywhere—in the skyrocketing increase of Satanism and cults, in genocide (which have been many in just the last century), and in the steeply increasing rates of contemporary suicides, homicides, and sexual trafficking and violence. Do you think this rise in evil is attributable solely to ourselves,

---

[46] This is the view of J. R. R. Tolkien. See Joseph Pearce, "J. R. R. Tolkien: Truth and Myth," Catholic Education Resource Center, https://www.catholiceducation.org/en/culture/art/j-r-r-tolkien-truth-and-myth.html.

[47] Carl Jung, *Children's Dreams: Notes from the Seminar Given in 1936–1940*, ed. Lorenz Jung and Maria Meyer-Grass (Princeton: Princeton University Press, 2010), chap 1.

or was it partly inspired—malevolently? I don't think it's crazy to believe in a spiritual influence for evil. I think it's quite rational to admit that there may be spiritual beings who have it in for us. If that's so, they would try not only to overtly tempt us (by making suggestions to our imagination and unconscious mind) but also to deceive us—to lead us away from what would really make us happy and toward what would really make us miserable.

But, whether you believe in evil spirits or not, it's a good idea to examine your own thoughts and impulses *as if* evil spirits were real. Call it a metaphor if you like. The important point to remember is that forces exist that will try to steer you wrong, away from what will ultimately lead you to happiness. You need to learn to recognize when that's happening because those forces can be subtle: "Even Satan disguises himself as an angel of light," said St. Paul (2 Cor. 11:14).

So, if an angel of light comes to you, how do you know whether it's the wrong kind of angel?

First, we should remember the three great virtues: faith, hope, and love. Those are the three virtues that lead us toward good and away from evil, toward happiness and away from misery. They give us a rule that's fairly simple to state, though it's not always easy to implement: If something leads to more faith, hope, and love *in the long term*, then it's probably a good inspiration (from a good angel or the Holy Spirit). If something leads to less faith, hope, and love in the long term, it's probably a bad inspiration (from an evil spirit).

Why would evil spirits try to disguise themselves as good spirits? From a Christian perspective, they do so because he has tried to overtly tempt you to go against your conscience or your religion's principles, but you've been resisting them. After a while they change tactics and try deceit instead. They come to you with a seemingly good suggestion (posing as a good angel or the Holy Spirit) but exaggerate it to the point that you are almost sure to fail. When you do, you may fall away from your Level 4 spiritual/transcendent path in discouragement—and even revert back to a Level 1 or 2 path. The evil spirits know that this will lead to misery, and (they hope) also to despair.

For example, you might feel a sudden inspiration and decide that you'll be more involved in church. Great! You end up on half a dozen committees. You're running the parish festival. You're volunteering to paint the social hall this weekend. And your kids are failing in middle school, and your wife has stopped going to church with you, and your whole family seems sullen and resentful at the dinner table. You begin to think that God doesn't care about you at all. Look what you did for God and look at the result!

Well, you did something that seemed really good, but the result was *less* faith, *less* hope, and *less* love for your family, and as a result, for you. That was not a good inspiration. From a Christian perspective, it was Satan in the angel-of-light suit giving you a really bad idea that *appeared* to be a good idea. It's good to be involved with your faith community, but it's important to know when doing too much of a good thing is having bad effects on your own happiness and the happiness of people around you.

Notice that the evil spirit has left out something vital: your family is also your vocation. You have duties to your spouse and your children. By giving you *half* the picture, the evil spirit appeals to the good part of your nature and leads you away from the proper balance that would really make you happy.

As Aristotle would tell you, moderation is important even in good things because many vices are just virtues pushed to extremes.

Now, it would have been great to know beforehand what was going to happen, wouldn't it? But that isn't always possible. You need to be adaptable. You can't stubbornly follow one course you've decided on as the evidence mounts that it was a disaster.

However, you can get better at making these discernments so that you spare yourself some of the bad effects of wrong turns in the future. One thing you can do is learn some of Satan's tricks — or, if you prefer, the malevolent quirks of your own unconscious.

Rationalizations are at the top of the list of deceits. If something would normally disturb your conscience, but you can think of a good reason why it shouldn't, then you might be a victim of rationalization. It isn't *really* lying if it gets the right candidate elected. Everybody else cuts corners in this business: that's what people expect. We pay too much in taxes anyway, so . . .

Your mind is really good at coming up with these self-justifications. They just roll out, one after another, almost as if somebody were whispering them in your ear — or is a voice really there?

But, if we're so good at rationalizing, how will we even recognize when we're doing it? Rationalizing generally happens when you want to excuse yourself for trying to get away with something. You feel as though there's a higher standard, but it's okay if you don't meet it because . . . and your mind fills in all sorts of reasons.

These rationalizations happen especially to people who haven't yet made the leap of faith to the fourth level. If you *have* made that leap of faith, you're more likely to be conscious of them because you're already trying to see the larger picture.

Remember that you have something else to watch out for. We've seen how the evil presence can use unrealistically high standards to deceive you, then discourage you, and incite you to return to the misery of Level 1 and 2.

"So," you think, "evil gets me coming and going! How can I sort out these impulses if even the good ones can be deceptions?"

Once again, the beacons of faith, hope, and love guide you. They cut through both the rationalizations and the unrealistically high standards. Ask whether this will lead to more faith, hope, and love for everyone in the long term, and look out for unconsidered factors—your family, for example, which is so close to you that you might not even have thought about it, just as people who live on a mountain can forget about the mountain.

All this gives us some clues to look for when we're troubleshooting inspiration in our happiness quest. You've been climbing the ladder of happiness. You made that leap of faith to the fourth rung. You started really changing your life, and at first it felt as though you were really making a difference. But now you find yourself falling into misery again. You feel as though it was all a mistake. Maybe God doesn't care about us after all.

When you realize that your trust in God, your hope in salvation, your ability to love, and the positive outlook from your spiritual life are being clouded or even engulfed with discouragement, *stop!* The presence of an evil spirit posing as an angel of light may be in the picture. Look back in your memory and try to think how you got here. You'll probably find it was some decision you made that seemed like a really good idea when you made it. And I'm guessing that it was a decision that you thought would speed up the process of getting to happiness.

Did you see a video on YouTube about how you can deepen your spiritual life with some particular devotion? Did you meet someone who spends three hours a day in prayer and think, "I should do that, too"? Did you see a call for volunteers in the parish and think, "They need me, even if I'm already stretched pretty thin"?

If your decision to pursue a course of action led to an increase in misery for yourself and the people around you and decreased faith, hope, love, and the positive outlook from your spiritual life, then reevaluate and modify your course of action. You were probably deceived, and the way out is to modify your course of action—or find a better course of action.

I've spent a lot of time on this part of the subject—maybe too much—because I want to make it clear that there are some traps you can fall into. But that's true of anything worth doing. It's especially true when you've made that leap of faith to the fourth level, because you're going against the cultural flow today. You may face opposition from both the forces of evil and the forces of why-can't-you-be-normal.

So you may occasionally have to backtrack, telling yourself honestly that you made a bad decision, and go back to that last intersection and take the other road. But that's progress. You've learned something about yourself and what it will take to reach your destination.

St. Ignatius of Loyola made quite a study of the discernment of spirits, and his first rule is very instructive: *Never make an important decision when you're in a state of desolation.* By *desolation* he meant not only a bleak or depressing emotional condition but also a decrease in faith, hope, love, and the positive outlook from your spiritual life. These negative emotions and states of mind can open the door to being deceived about your spiritual path, regardless of whether this results from an evil spirit or your own imperfect mental processes.

Of course, there are times when you can't help making a decision at your lowest point. It may be a decision that needs to be made right now. I understand, and I have two bits of advice.

First, ask for help. I'd suggest a good spiritual director or a wise clergyman. If one is not available, then a psychologist can help too. It's best to have someone who's in sympathy with your ongoing spiritual quest, but who can see you from the outside and look at your life more objectively than you can. However, if you're desperate, being able to talk the issue over with a nonprofessional friend or family member who has objectivity and shares your spiritual views can be quite helpful.

Second, assume that things will get better. When we're at a low point, we're strongly tempted to despair: we make the assumption that things will always be this bad, or that they'll get worse, and the downward track will never end. *That assumption is false,* unless you make it true by your own actions. Make your decisions based on the assumption that things will get better, even if you can't see how. This is especially important if you're an intellectual type, because when you're depressed, your mind will be working overtime to come up with reasons why you *should* be depressed. You may just have to set reason aside for a little while and have unreasoning faith in a spiritual reality capable of bringing light from the darkness. But you can console the reasoning part of your mind with the knowledge that evidence backs up this assumption, as we have seen in chapters 11–12.

Be Ready for the Spirit

Now that we've spent all this time considering what to beware of, we can think about what real inspiration looks like. You'll notice things that seem to be pushing you or pulling you toward what you ought to do. Just as it made sense to assume evil spirits as a *metaphor,* even if you don't believe in them as actual beings, it also makes sense to assume *divine providence* — the guidance of God that moves through all our lives. This is particularly important in times of challenge and suffering. What does divine providence look like?

First of all, we have to remember that God is concerned with all of us. Much as I might like to be His favorite, I'm not. God's love extends to every one of His creations, and therefore His providence has to look out for everybody. What that means for us is that we can't expect God to push through our specific desires when they interfere with the good of other people. If it seems as though you're not getting what you want, remember that there are other people in the world too. What I can tell you, though, is that in the long term what is best for everyone will be best for your own happiness. You can't possibly know all the circumstances of the world around you, so you may not be able to see right now how a particular difficult situation is going to be for your benefit. But that's why faith is needed.

Second, we also have to remember that we have *free will*. Our freedom is so important that God lets us do the wrong thing, even if it leads us to misery. We've mentioned this principle before, but it's worth going over again: love isn't love unless it's freely chosen. If you don't have the possibility of choosing something that is *not* loving, then you are either forced to love or programmed to love. In either case, the love is not *your own* but the will of the enforcer or programmer. Without freedom—without our good and loving deeds originating from our choice—there would be no purpose to our existence beyond that of a highly trained chimpanzee. But that freedom comes at the price that we can mess up our lives and others' lives badly, and God won't stop us.

What God will do, though, is send us signs that we're messing up, so that we can freely change course before it's too late. God will also send us signs that show us what the right course would be, so that we have everything we need for success if we decide to take Him up on the offer.

If we put our faith in God's providence, we'll be ready to work *with* God's plan instead of against it. That's the attitude we need to have in order to be able to recognize His guidance.

What we *don't* need is to think we can figure it all out. Prayer is good, but sometimes praying for specific things leads to disappointment and distrust.

That isn't to say that you should never pour out your heart to God and tell Him what you really want. What you're asking for may be consistent with His will. Hence, you should go ahead and do it. But remember the example of Jesus.

Do you remember His prayer in the Garden of Gethsemane? We Christians call it "the agony in the garden." Jesus knew He was about to be arrested. He knew that the arrest could only lead to one result: crucifixion. So He went to the Garden of Gethsemane, just a short walk outside Jerusalem, with His disciples; and then He left the disciples alone for a few minutes and went off by Himself to pray: "My Father, if it be possible, let this cup [of suffering] pass from me; nevertheless, not as I will, but as you will" (Matt. 26:39). And a little bit later—after He had come back and found His disciples nodding off—He went back and prayed, "My Father, if this [cup of suffering] cannot pass unless I drink it, thy will be done" (Matt. 26:42).

Now, you notice that Jesus really didn't want to be crucified. He wasn't afraid to pray to His Father to get Him out of it if it were possible. Nevertheless, He added the one point we should all remember in our prayers: "Nevertheless, not as I will, but as you will."

That's the important clause that many of us leave out. Or, worse, we unconsciously get it backwards: "Not as you will, but as I will." I know I've done that many times.

It's easy to do that when you're praying. You might have real faith, and you know God is all-powerful, so of course He can give you what you want, right? Or, more subtly, you might be unconsciously testing God: if He gives you what you want, then you know He's there.

When I was younger, I made that mistake frequently. "Here's what I need to get out of this challenging predicament," I told God. "Just do this, and everything will be fine." And then if it didn't happen that way, I explained it to Him more precisely and with a preferred timetable. If He still did not comply with my very reasonable suggestions, I was baffled by God's "failure" to answer my prayers, especially after I'd taken the trouble to give Him an itemized list of what I needed.

I've known many people who have gone through some of the worst experiences you can imagine—for example, parents who have lost a child. Can any mother or father even imagine anything worse than that? Think of how many seemingly unanswered prayers there must have been. And yet some of those people came through that cross with stronger faith. Why? They came to understand the big picture. They understood what we all know intellectually but have a hard time processing emotionally: that *all* life on earth is temporary. Life after death is really our only hope—but what a hope it is! Sometimes a loss like that leads to a firmer grasp of the truth that life continues after the earthly existence has ended. And that deeper awareness can lead to a better and more joyful earthly existence.

God wants us to cooperate with His way, which is always oriented toward *eternal* life for *everyone* within the bounds of human *freedom*. What that means is that God will show us what His plan is, within the limits of our freedom and understanding, if we'll just pay attention. The Spirit uses our experiences and our emotional states to give us guidance, and if we're willing to accept that guidance, we can shorten our journey to happiness.

So what does that guidance look like?

It often comes as some sort of jolt that kicks us out of the rut we're in. This jolt can be a sudden opportunity or a sudden onset of suffering.

"Wait a minute," you might say. "Suffering? You mean God would allow me to suffer just to send a message?"

Yes, if that's the best way to get through to you.

What this means is that suffering is one of the elements you should pay attention to when you're trying to find your way forward.

Redemptive Suffering

One of the points you'll hear religious folks talking about is the "redemptive" quality of suffering. It's not unique to Christians either. People in other religions also talk about how suffering can be a good thing. You'll hear Buddhists, for example, talk about it as strong medicine.

How can that be true? Isn't suffering pretty much the definition of a bad thing? Are these people just masochists or what?

Well, I will tell you a secret. I don't enjoy suffering any more than you do. Unpleasant things are as unpleasant to me as they are to you. I don't like getting sick or getting hurt or going blind. I don't like losing friends. I don't like having financial worries. None of the experiences we think of as "suffering" are my idea of a good time.

But sometimes suffering is good for us. We recognize that when it's a medical procedure. We may have to have surgery. We may have to have a tooth drilled. We may have to swallow medicine that tastes really bad. We don't like any of those experiences. But we go through them because we know it will be worse if we don't. We know that our lives will be better because of the suffering we have to endure right now.

That's true of a lot more things than trips to the dentist. Suffering can wake us up and take us out of ourselves and our obsessions. It can tell us what's really important to us and make us concentrate on that.

That first level of happiness is where a lot of our problems lie. We get locked into physical pleasures — food, sex, comfort — and neglect the things we really need. Suffering comes along and takes those physical pleasures away. Instead of collapsing or despairing, we need to use our faith perspective and ask, "Is God allowing this to help me out of a self-destructive situation? Is He trying to help me get off a path that is destructive to others?" If so, it is best to take the hint because it will be better for us in the long term.

The same is true of Level 2 happiness. It's easy to get stuck in the second level of desire, constantly playing the comparison game. Then suffering comes along, and we *lose*. We know we're not doing better than everybody else. It's painful to realize that, especially in our modern world where schools and marketers and all the other social forces are constantly telling us to compare ourselves to the people around us. But if that's what was keeping us from moving on to a higher level of happiness, then suffering is what we need.

That's the secret of some of the happiest people you know. You've seen them. They're the people suffering from terminal diseases, the people who have nothing but the clothes on their backs, the people who know they've lost everything. But they're happy. They greet you with a smile. They ask you how things are going for *you*, and they're genuinely happy if you say you're doing pretty well. How is it possible for these people to be so cheerful?

They've learned the secret: suffering can produce joy.

It's not a masochistic joy at all. They're not enjoying the suffering. They find their joy in the things they would have missed if they were still caught up in themselves. Their suffering has allowed them to move up the ladder of happiness, past the easy material and egocentric pleasures that sometimes stand in our way.

So I hope this little digression about suffering has given you some appreciation for how suffering can be a good thing, even when we don't like it at the time. First, remember God's goal *is* to alleviate our suffering, but that's not His sole mission. He wants to alleviate our suffering in a way that will lead to eternal life not only for us but for everyone, within the bounds of our freedom. This will help us pray the prayer of suffering given to us by Jesus: "My Father, if it be possible, let this cup [of suffering] pass from me; nevertheless, not as I will, but as you will."

Then you need to pay attention to the message suffering might be bringing you. What is it depriving you of? Is that something you *needed* to be deprived of? Or is that deprivation opening up some new avenue that you haven't explored yet? These are questions to consider honestly and patiently when you're having a bad time or even when catastrophe strikes. Doing so may help you onto the path of higher happiness — or even onto the path of highest happiness throughout eternity.

The Good, the Bad, and the Indifferent

The fact is that there will be good times and bad times in every life, and a whole lot of times that aren't really either good or bad — just neutral. The Spirit comes to us in different ways depending on where we are in life. And, I should add, so does the wrong kind of spirit.

For the bad times, I'm going to start with a story from my own life.

I was meant to be a lawyer — at least, that was what my whole early life seemed to be telling me. My father had a very successful law firm, and I would study law and go to work with my father's firm, and everything would be set. I wouldn't have to worry about my career path, and my father would have a son he could be proud of and rely on to keep the firm going.

But I kept finding myself fascinated by philosophy and theology. I could understand the law, but it didn't give me the sense of overwhelming inspiration that reading one of the great theologians or philosophers gave me. Eventually, I realized this was a sign that my real mission was somewhere other than my father's law firm. And an opportunity came up that led me down the path I ultimately took—into the seminary and the priesthood.

On the way there, though, there was a big fat bump in the road.

I was studying in Rome, and it was less than a year before my ordination. I had been noticing that I was having more and more trouble making out the little dots under Hebrew letters that indicate the vowels. Those little dots are important, so I went to an eye doctor thinking I needed better glasses. He told me the bad news: I had retinitis pigmentosa, a disease of the retina that was only going to get worse. It would gradually take away my ability to read fine print, and then bigger print. I wouldn't be able to drive.

What good would a blind priest be to the Church?

You can probably guess how depressed I was. I was convinced that this was a sign from God that I wasn't on the right path. I was ready to tell my superiors that I had to bow out and give up. And at that moment, when I had hit bottom, I ran into just the person I would have to break the bad news to: my provincial, the head of my province in the Jesuits.

I told him the bad news—that I was damaged goods and that if he needed to dismiss me from the order, I would completely understand.

He looked at me and asked, "Bob, what spirit have *you* been listening to?"

It completely turned the situation on its head. I had received a message from an angel of light, but it was just a clever disguise. My provincial told me he was sure that Satan had planted this despair in my mind. I would find a way forward, and I was meant for the priesthood.

And he was right. After that, things started to fall into place, and they've been falling into place ever since. I *did* progressively lose my sight—and it hasn't slowed me down a bit. Whenever I needed help, there was always someone to drive me, to type for me, to do whatever I needed so that God's purpose for me could be accomplished.

What happened was something I've learned to recognize in the activity of the Spirit. When I was at rock bottom, I happened *just coincidentally* to run into the one person who could put me back on my feet and set me on the right path again. But I don't think it's coincidence at all. I see a pattern here. This is how God's providence works in my life and in the lives of countless other people I've known. When you're feeling low, and you don't see any way forward, and you run into someone who sees your position from a radically different point of view, *pay attention.* This may be the guidance you were looking for.

What did I do then? Well, I'll tell you what I didn't do. I didn't come up with a detailed plan for how I would overcome every difficulty posed by my degenerating sight. I couldn't. In fact, I still had no idea how I was going to overcome some of those difficulties. Instead, I just recognized that God was with me here, and I learned to trust that there would be guidance when I needed it. And there was.

This was especially hard for me because I've always been a planner. I've always figured that the world belongs to the prepared. If I didn't know what I was going to do next, I felt very uneasy. But the news about my retinitis pigmentosa shook me out of that. It taught me that I can't make a plan for every contingency—because, I can tell you, none of my plans had considered the contingency that I might go blind. That was a challenge, but it was what I needed to make me trust in God to get me through, even if I didn't have a backup plan.

I think my own experience changed a lot more than that. I was pretty arrogant before I had that eye problem. I didn't see it myself, but other people saw it—people who were too polite to say anything. I had to get over that in a hurry. I had to learn that whatever accomplishments I counted as mine weren't really *my* accomplishments. God gave me a problem that would cause me to need help every step of the way, and I'd have to get over my pride and realize that whatever I did, it was only through His help. And I had to trust that God *would* give me that help.

This trust (along with humble love) is one of the main lessons the Spirit will try to teach you. I don't mean that you should never make any plans for the future. You have to make appointments and register for classes and all those other things that make you a functioning human being in civilized society. But be adaptable. Listen to the guidance you get.

You'll also get guidance when things are going well for you, so learn to recognize and look for that kind of guidance too. It might be something that tells you you're on the right track: you suddenly find an opportunity opening up in your job, for example. Or it might be a chance to change direction. I told you how that opportunity came up for me when I was a young man planning a career in law. Things were going very well for me then, but I had a chance to do what I really loved, and I followed that guidance.

Then there will be times when things are just poking along, not really great and not really bad, and something comes up that makes you realize you have a talent you didn't know about or a chance to do something you hadn't thought about doing before. Maybe you've always liked drawing and suddenly the agency you work for needs an illustrator for a panic project, and the boss asks, "Is there anyone around here who can draw? Anyone?" Maybe there's a chance to build your gardening hobby into an urban-farm project that gives inner-city teenagers a chance to spend their afternoons growing something delicious.

But how do you know whether this is really the right step?

How Do I Know?

The first thing to do is take the first step in what seems to be a likely direction. If you have a new opportunity, make a move in that direction. If something you've been doing seems to have been bringing you misery, take a step away from it.

Now watch what happens in your own mind.

Do you feel a sense of peace and contentment? A feeling that you're where you ought to be? Do you have an increase in trust in God, hope in your salvation, and the capacity for love? Through the lens of your faith, is your view of life positive? If so, this is probably the good Spirit telling you that you're headed in the right direction. Another point to look out for: Did this first step open up opportunities for more steps? Does it seem like you've broken through a logjam and cleared the way forward to new and exciting endeavors? These are all good signs that you're doing what you're supposed to be doing, and you should do more of it.

Or, on the other hand, do you feel as though you're falling back into the pit of misery? Are you experiencing decreased trust in God, hope in your salvation, and capacity for love? Is your lens of faith becoming more obscure? If so, this is probably the Spirit telling you you're headed in the *wrong* direction.

Just as pleasure and pain lead us and all animals toward what we need and away from what we must avoid, the Spirit uses these feelings of *consolation* and *desolation* to lead us toward the things that are good for our spiritual life and away from those that are damaging.

And what if you don't feel anything at all? Well, that may be a sign too. It may not be time to make a decision yet. Keep your options open and watch out for more signs.

In any case, we need to approach these changes patiently. Sometimes you do get a very definite, very positive sign all at once, but more often you learn by observing the incremental changes in your way of thinking and feeling. It might help to write down just a few thoughts every day. I don't necessarily mean that you should keep a journal, the way your high school English teacher wanted you to do. But if you can just write three lines about what you've done and how you feel about it, you'll have a record of what your mental state was. Then, after a couple of months, look back at how you felt when you first started down this path. Do you see an *increase* in trust, hope, and love since then? If so, you're probably doing the right thing: it looks as though God is guiding you down this path. Or do you see an overall *decrease* in trust, hope, and love? Then you may have been deceived, and you should candidly reconsider what you're doing and whether it's for the best.

And there's always the possibility, once again, that you don't notice much change—that you're stuck in neutral. In that case, I'd recommend persisting in what you're doing. But monitor your mental state and your behavior. There are, after all, some times when one course isn't any better than another, but not any worse either. However, if you start to see a turn upward or downward in the trust, hope, and love department, act on what you observe and let it guide your decisions.

Remember that God won't *make* you do anything you don't want to do. God respects your freedom: you have to decide that you want to follow the guidance you've been receiving. If your decision is to keep wandering down the same path, in spite of the indications that it's leading you to misery, then you can do that. God will give you guidance, but He won't force you to be happy.

However, you've already taken a big step. You've started to think about what would make you genuinely happy and how to get there. Follow through, and you'll reach your goal. And ask for God's help along the way. You can be sure you'll get it if your path is consistent with His will.

How do we ask for God's help? Good question. This is where we have to learn a little about how prayer works.

15

About Prayer

In addition to attending church services and following divine providence, the third point I mentioned about living on Level 4 is prayer. Of course you'll be praying in church, but I mean that you need to pray privately and personally as well. You need to make it a habit.

Why prayer? Isn't that a little superstitious? God knows what we need, right? If God is all-powerful and all-knowing, then what could we tell Him that He doesn't already know?

I can imagine a lot of people having that reaction to the suggestion that they should pray. But I think they're misunderstanding the purpose of prayer.

Think of your human relationships. When you were young, your mother probably knew what you really needed. She knew how much food you needed to eat, she knew when you were growing out of your clothes and needed new ones, she knew when it was time to get you off to school, and she knew when you were sick.

Does that mean she never wanted you to talk to her? Of course not.

The same goes for your husband or wife if you're married. After you've lived together for a few years, you know each other pretty well. You could probably go for days at a time without having any essential information to convey because each of you knows what the other needs, even to some extent what the other is thinking. But that doesn't mean you don't want to talk. In fact, if the person you're married to isn't talking to you, that's a sign that something is really wrong, isn't it?

The reason we talk is not just to hand practical bits of information to each other. We talk to *communicate* — to share experiences, to reassure each other, to make our relationships grow. We talk to be part of each other's lives. Remember, no man is an island.

Now, you'll remember that we were going to try to form a *relationship* with God. This is what we really want to get from stepping up to the fourth level. When we pray, that's what we're doing. We may ask for things from God. We may even plead for things if we feel desperate. But when we pray, we're primarily forming a relationship.

How do you get started praying if you haven't been in the habit?

I encourage you to learn more of the traditional prayers and devotions of your faith tradition — although I'd caution you not to delve into too much at once and set yourself up for failure. Pick one devotion that you feel puts you closer to God and work that into your life. You're on your way.

We talked about building our relationship with God as a *person*, and about how that means *communicating* with God. Now we're going to dig a little deeper into what that means because prayer isn't just something you're born knowing how to do. Just as when we communicate with people, it's a skill. Like any other activity worth doing, the more you learn about it, the more you'll get out of it, and the more you'll look forward to those times in the day when you get to sit down and talk with God.

You're not born knowing how to speak. You pick up speech by constantly practicing the skill. You hear your parents and family talk all day. You hear other people talking when you go out into the world. You hear talking on the television or the radio or the computer. You imitate what you hear, and you get responses to what you say, and gradually you learn how to express your thoughts to another person.

If you learn a foreign language later in life, it can be harder than learning the language you grew up with. But the principle is the same. Learning a foreign language works best through constant practice. This is why people who are serious about learning a new language usually take "immersion" courses—courses where you speak the language constantly—and then find as many opportunities as they can to listen to and speak the new language.

Prayer is like that. When you were young, if you grew up in a religious family, you probably learned a few rote prayers. You may never have learned anything more about praying than those. And they're not a bad start. But they're just a start. They're like the alphabet song: they help you remember the things you need to know to be able to pray. Then you go on with that knowledge, and if you keep practicing, you'll get really good at praying.

What we're going to try to do now is move beyond the alphabet song. We'll divide up the task into three kinds of praying:

1. *Contemplative prayer*, which is where we open the lines of communication with God.
2. *Divine guidance*, where we ask for God to help us through our struggle toward our ultimate goal, which is happiness.
3. *Interior transformation*, which is where we use a self-examining prayer to find what's wrong in our minds and hearts and get on the road to straightening it out. This one sounds scary, but it's going to be worth the work, I promise you.

The Four Levels of Happiness

Before we go any further, though, we're going to ask ourselves an important question. It's important because it will determine how well we pray, or even whether we're able to continue praying.

How Do You Think about God?

How do you think about God? It's a question you should consider for a while, because there may be two different answers to it: the answer that you think I want to hear and the answer that's really true.

You probably think I want to hear that you think of God as a loving Father. Well, I would be very happy if you did. If we all thought of God as a loving Father, we'd all be a lot happier. But I suspect many of us have a different view.

Let me tell you my own experience. I was a faithful Catholic Christian. I was more than that: I was in my novitiate, so I was planning on a lifelong devotion to God.

Yet I was having trouble praying. I could go through all the motions, yes. But when time for evening prayer came around, I had stuff to do. There were things that suddenly had to be accomplished and couldn't wait. "Look at this room," I'd tell myself. "It's a mess! I'd better do something about that." When I said, "I really have to do laundry right now," I knew I was dodging.

I finally realized I was finding any excuse to put off an encounter with God. Why was that?

I was afraid.

Now, I would have told you that I believed God was my loving Father. And in a certain intellectual sense, that was true. But that wasn't the image in my mind when I was getting ready to pray. I saw a different kind of God. The God I imagined was disgusted with me. I wasn't living up to my potential. I was a sinner. I was a disappointment.

These notions of God kept me from having the kind of relationship with God that He wanted me to have. I dreaded prayer, precisely because it *was* an encounter with God, and I was afraid to face my idea of God.

When I realized that, I also realized that there was only one good way out. I asked God for help. When I did pray, I said, "Help me see You the way You really are."

And that did it.

My incredible novice master figured out that I might be having this problem and asked what my view of God was like. When he prodded it out of me, my view was somewhere between the "disgusted god," the "angry god," and the "payback god." He indicated to me that this was *not* the God of Jesus Christ.

Being a practical lad, I said, "Well, do you have a couple of Scripture passages that'll clue me in to who God *really* is?" He responded that he had a very good one, which was Jesus' definitive revelation about His Father. I said, "I don't think I remember that passage. What is it?" He said, "It's the parable of the prodigal son. What do you think that Jesus meant by the father in that story?" I paused for a moment and responded, "Jesus' Father—God?" He said with a smile, "How perceptive of you."

He gave me a summary of the story to use for my prayer over the next month. I'll give this summary in a bit, but for the moment, suffice it to say that as I compared the father of the prodigal son (Jesus' image of God) to my distorted images of God, my images began to dissipate, and my prayer was transformed from the prayer of misery to the prayer of relationship, gratitude, and love.

But before I get to that summary, I need to discuss some of the distorted images of God prevalent in our culture.

Some of us see an "angry god"—a god who is just furious that we haven't lived up to his expectations. The angry god is just waiting for us to sit down and pray so he can really tell us off. You may remember some truly cruel people who scared you so much that you could not function. If that's your image of God, prayer will be virtually impossible.

Or there's the "payback god." The payback god is even worse: he's keeping a list of every little thing we've done wrong, and he's going to make sure we get what's coming to us for every single one of them. When we pray to him, we feel like there'll be a lightning strike of punishment right around the corner—a threat to our job, our reputation, our spouse and children, or some other crucial part of our life. Or we can attribute our present suffering to this revengeful god paying us back for past sins: "The reason I'm suffering now is because God has been waiting for just the right moment to pay me back, and now when I'm most vulnerable, he's decided, 'It's payback time!' " If you are praying to this god, you'll no doubt be expecting retribution for past and present wrongs. Don't expect mercy or compassion—get ready to duck!

Then there's the "stoic god." Stoicism was a philosophical system that started in ancient Greece, and it has had a profound influence on Western thought. The stoic god ignores our prayers, because we do not matter much in the great scheme of things. This god expects us to handle sufferings in life with indifference and courage. His basic response is, "Buck up—I'm sick and tired of your whining! Turn a granite face to the world, and just remember, 'What doesn't kill you makes you stronger!' " This god is not only indifferent to you but disgusted with your victim attitude. If you're praying to him, don't expect a sympathetic ear or a helping hand, or anything to do with love—get ready for a severe repudiation of your weakness.

All kinds of different images of God can get stuck in our heads. Some see God as a competitor, jealous of our accomplishments and waiting to take them away from us. Some see God as just disgusted, turning His face away from us because He's ashamed to be associated with us.

These images of God affect our prayer life deeply. How could they not? The way you imagine God determines how your relationship with Him will go, just as the way you imagine a friend determines how your relationship with that person will go. If you start to think of your friend as always annoyed, or always vengeful, or cold and uncaring, then, of course, you'll start avoiding that friend, and pretty soon you won't be friends anymore.

No matter what kind of home we may have been raised in, Jesus' definitive teaching about who God (His Father) is can help us immensely in overcoming false and distorted ideas of God. As I said, this happened to me, thanks to my novice master who gave me a summary of the parable of the prodigal son. Remember the father in this story is Jesus' definitive revelation of who God (His Father) is.

Once there was a father who had two sons, and the younger of them rejected and disgraced the man by telling him he meant nothing to him except for his money. The son asked for his inheritance before his older brother (disgracing him too). He then went to a foreign land—the Gentiles—where he rejected his people, his Jewish covenant, and his country. Then he spent all the money on dissolute living (violating the Law and his relationship with God again, and again, and again). Finally, in poverty, he was consigned to a Gentile farm to live with the pigs (making himself impure for the rest of his life—touching a pig was bad enough!). In other words, according to Jesus, this boy, by first-century Jewish standards, could *not* have been worse. His audience would have thought that the father *should* disown him.

But that's not what happened. After the boy tells his father, "I have sinned against you and no longer deserve to be called your son; just treat me as one of the servants," his father has a completely unexpected reaction (remember, the father in this story is God the Father, according to Jesus). The father throws his arms around his son and kisses him (because his love for him has not changed despite the son's many transgressions). He then tells the servants to put a robe on his son (to treat him like royalty) and sandals on his feet (elevating him from the status of slave to free man), then gives him the family ring (with the family signet on it, indicating that he is a full-fledged member of the family once again—without restriction). Finally, he orders the servants to kill the fatted calf (the best animal on the farm) for a feast because he is overjoyed to have his son back.

So what is Jesus saying about God His Father? He is perfectly merciful, compassionate, healing, and protective. Instead of being angry, retributive, and dominating, He restores dignity and what was lost through sin. In sum, He is perfectly loving.

This parable is a great light to correct our minds and hearts not only at the beginning of our prayer lives but any time we begin to drift into false images of God—e.g., the angry god, the payback god, the stoic god, the disgusted god, and so forth. Recall from the previous chapter that the Holy Spirit wants you to increase in trust, hope, and love, while the evil spirit wants precisely the opposite. This means that the Holy Spirit is pointing to God as the father of the prodigal son, while the evil spirit is pointing to the false and distorted ideas of God. I would recommend keeping this summary of the parable of the prodigal son with you when you start praying until Jesus' view of God His Father becomes familiar. A painting of the prodigal son's father may also prove helpful. I recommend Rembrandt's.

Jesus' revelation of His Father's heart (as well as His own) has really transformed my prayer life. Instead of avoiding prayer, I look forward, as St. Teresa of Avila said, to conversing with the One who loves me.

A perfectly loving Father would love us *no matter what*. This is not to say that He would not want us to change our ways if we are undermining ourselves and others—He does. But whatever happens, He doesn't stop loving us.

If concepts speak more clearly to you than parables, you might try another approach to the perfect love of God that many have found useful—St. Paul's hymn to love in 1 Corinthians 13. Let's start with the hymn as it is written:

> Love is patient and kind; love is not jealous or boastful; it is not arrogant or rude. Love does not insist on its own way; it is not irritable or resentful; it does not rejoice at wrong, but rejoices in the right. Love bears all things, believes all things, hopes all things, endures all things. Love never ends. (1 Cor. 13:4-8)

To emphasize Jesus' prioritization of love above all other virtues, laws, and spiritual charisms, Paul adds, "If I have prophetic powers, and understand all mysteries and all knowledge, and if I have all faith, so as to remove mountains, but have not love, I am nothing" (1 Cor. 13:2).

Now, recalling that God is perfect love (from the prodigal son's father), replace the word *love* with *God* in the Corinthians hymn:

God is patient and kind.

God is not jealous or boastful. God is not your rival.

God is not arrogant or rude. If you talk to God, God will listen and care about what you have to say.

God is not irritable or resentful. He is peace-filled and forgiving.

God does not rejoice in wrong but rejoices in the right. Remember that God made you good, and God knows and rejoices in the good in you—even when you can't see it in yourself.

God bears all things, believes all things, hopes all things, endures all things. You can't push God to the limit of His patience, because there is no limit to God's patience.

God's love never ends. You will always have God to rely on. He will never turn His back on you, even if you think you've really made a mess of your life.

Read over that short section from Paul's letter a few times, and each time tell yourself that *this is what God is like.* Try to form that image of God in your mind: always loving, always patient, always ready to listen to you, and always happy that you want to have a conversation. *That's* the God you're praying to.

Here's another point to think about when you're forming your mental image of God. We say, "God the Father," which is an accurate way of translating what the Greek books of the New Testament say. But *father* is a very formal word in English. Most people these days don't call their own fathers "Father" when they're talking to them. In fact, if you hear your neighbor address someone else as "Father," you probably assume he's talking to a priest.

Jesus called His Father "Abba" (see Mark 14:36). St. Paul tells us that Jesus' followers in His time did the same: "We call out, 'Abba! Father!'" (Rom. 8:15).

Abba is the Hebrew and Aramaic word that means "Dad" or "Daddy." That is, it's the affectionate, but still respectful, term you would use for your own father if you were a child.

Think about that for a while. Jesus and Paul think we should call God "Dad" or "Daddy." *That's* the kind of relationship we're supposed to have with God.

If you believe that Jesus is the Word of God (John 1:1)—or you're at least open to Jesus' teaching that love is the highest virtue, and, therefore, God is love—then this is the image of God you'll want to have in your prayer. More importantly, this is the reality of God with whom you are entering into relationship during your prayer.

I know just *saying* these things isn't going to change your mental image of God right away. It would be great if I could do that for you, but we all have a lot of baggage we're carrying with us from years of the wrong attitudes. Still, you can start the change now. Every time you pray, think about the God you're praying to. When you catch yourself thinking, "God doesn't care about me," "God has it in for me," or anything like that, go back and read the hymn to love in 1 Corinthians 13 or the parable of the prodigal son (Luke 15:11-32).

Then start to pray.

"But what will I say?" you might wonder. "What will I pray about?"

These are natural questions. Once when I was young, I met some big-deal celebrity writer at a book signing. I remember my mother telling me, "Go up and talk to him." Well, that was an easy thing to tell me to do, but what would I say? I was too timid to say anything.

This is where you have an advantage if you learned some of those rote prayers that parents teach their children. If not, it's easy to learn now. Then you have something to break the ice. You have things you can say to God. But this time, instead of just repeating the prayers from memory, you can think about the words and contemplate what they really mean.

Prayer as Conversation with the One Who Loves Us

The most important point about prayer is connecting with the One who loves you, and so it is essential at the beginning of any prayer—no matter how short—to call to mind the transcendent reality you are addressing. Whatever your religious tradition or spiritual framework, try at the beginning to connect with the sacred transcendent reality that many contemporary philosophers have given evidence of—the unrestricted intelligence present to our consciousness who is perfect love, justice, and beauty (see chapter 11). You might also call to mind the loving white light that many thousands of patients witnessed on "the other side" in their near-death experiences (see the description in chapter 12, e.g., Linda Stewart). If you are a Christian, call to mind the father in the parable of the prodigal son. Remember that the good and loving nature of the transcendent reality is one of the seven common characteristics of major world religions.[48]

Once you have connected with the sacred transcendent reality, you may want to begin with praying thoughtfully the words in some of the prayers you learned in your family or current religious community. These prayers will no doubt have something in common with the petitions of the Our Father, but they are different ways of expressing our need and love for God. If Jesus was right, then the sacred transcendent reality is present to you the minute you start praying. As Jesus teaches, God will not fail to listen, and He will answer according to His perfectly loving will for you.

What would you like to say to God? If you're anything like me, then you will probably take the conversation in one of three directions:

1. Prayers of petition
2. Prayers of gratitude, praise, and love
3. Prayers to become more like God and to avoid evil

[48] See Friedrich Heiler, "The History of Religions as a Preparation for the Cooperation of Religions," in *The History of Religions*, ed. Mircea Eliade and J. Kitagawa (Chicago: Chicago University Press, 1959).

Prayers of Petition

Remember, it's okay to ask God for what you need, even though He knows what you need before you ask. I frequently make recourse to brief and intense prayers of petition, but I try to add the prayer of Jesus in the Garden of Gethsemane—"Your loving will be done."

So for example, when we are in a financial pinch, I might pray, "Lord, please send some benefactors to help us, but if this is not Your will, then Your loving will be done." As I noted earlier, I avoid my old prayer in which I *tell* God what to do to alleviate my suffering, while offering an ideal timetable in which to complete the tasks. Fortunately, He has never seen fit to respond to this kind of prayer. The best kind of prayer is to ask for what you need, adding Jesus' caveat "if it is Your will."

We conclude with a starter list of some brief prayers of petition that can open the channel for God's help and consolation during times of suffering, foreboding, and fear:

❖ Lord make good come out of this suffering for me, my family and friends, others, and the world.

❖ Lord, I give up—You take care of it.

❖ Lord, push back this darkness and foreboding and whatever is causing it.

❖ Lord, I place my trust in You—cover me with Your protection.

❖ Lord, I offer up this suffering for the sake of others and the world.

❖ Lord, make good come out of whatever harm I might have caused.

❖ Thy loving will be done.

This last prayer is very effective during times of fear, suffering, temptation, and anger if we remember that God's will is loving. He desires nothing other than to optimize goodness, love, and salvation *for* you—and to do the same for others *through* you. In addition to prayers of petition for what you need, consider also prayers of petition for others—your family, friends, associates, and other acquaintances. As noted previously, praying for others really does help. It's an act of care for another person, which the Lord finds hard to resist. Indeed, He finds all acts of care hard to resist.

I have literally dozens of stories of efficacious prayers that produced highly unlikely healings and other beneficial turns of events. Were these improbable events caused by my prayers, others' prayers, or pure chance? I really don't know, but the frequency of these answered prayers leads me to believe that a loving providential hand is involved. Dr. Harold Koenig, Dr. Chester Tolson, and many others show a significant correlation between prayer and healing.[49] Prayers of petition do not end here.

The most universal prayer of petition is the Our Father, which asks the Lord to bring His kingdom, His loving will, our daily bread, forgiveness, and freedom from temptation and evil *to all of us*. The perfection of the Our Father is that it's not just for us or others we know but also for total strangers and the whole world. It is, as it were, a global act of compassion.

Prayers of Gratitude, Praise, and Love

Believe it or not, expressing gratitude, praise, and love really makes us happy—when we express this to other people or to God. There is

---

[49] See the research of Dr. Harold Koenig (Duke University Medical School) using a scientific methodology to draw a similar conclusion. See Dr. Harold Koenig et al., *Handbook of Religion and Health*, 3rd ed. (Oxford: Oxford University Press, 2023), 369-610. See also Dr. Chester Tolson and Dr. Harold Koenig, *The Healing Power of Prayer: The Surprising Connection between Prayer and Your Health* (Ada, MI: Baker Academic, 2004).

an old proverb that goes like this: "I never knew a person who was grateful and unhappy, or a person who was ungrateful and happy."

Grateful people take little for granted and feel blessed when others do almost anything for them. Ungrateful people take just about everything for granted and resent everything that they believed they deserved but did not get. As you know, resentment leads not only to anger but often to envy and hatred. In general, resentful, angry, envious, and hate-filled people are not that happy.

Unfortunately, Level 1 and 2 happiness tends to encourage egocentrism, ingratitude, and resentment. However, Level 3 and 4 happiness is premised on our genuine desire to make a positive difference to someone—including God—with our lives. In Levels 3 and 4 we actually come alive when we see someone benefit from our help, time, smile, advice, or listening—not because we feel superior by pitying them but because their happiness makes us happy—a genuine sense of loving empathy.

The same holds true for gratitude. Seeing someone come alive, benefit from, or take joy in our simple expression of appreciation or gratitude makes us happy. It not only gives us purpose but also brings us closer to that other person. It brings a spark of potential friendship or relationship.

The same holds true for God. When we express genuine gratitude to Him, we become happy because He is happy—He's the most appreciative being of all. Additionally, we draw closer to Him in sharing this happiness. We might say our relationship becomes more personal—He matters more to us, and we depend more on Him and commit more to Him. As this happens, He rubs off on us more, we become more like Him, and He allows us to see with ever greater intensity His love for us. We might say that the relationship grows in mutual affection and care so deeply that we find our home in Him, and He makes His home in us.

The same holds true for expressions of praise. Sometimes praise is a form of gratitude, but other times, it is a form of adoration, admiration, or worship of the sheer greatness, majesty, beauty, and glory of God's being. Like gratitude, when we praise the Lord for being the all-powerful, all-loving, all-beautiful Creator, we at once acknowledge our creatureliness while adoring His perfection and expressing loving adoration and worship. The Psalms, even though written twenty-six hundred years ago, are examples of this kind of praise and adoration. When we pray these prayers of loving adoration, it brings us closer and closer to the perfect mystery who has loved us into being.

Prayers to Become More like God and to Avoid Evil

In the next chapter, we will discuss this "Examen Prayer" more fully. For the moment, I want to bring to mind only two points:

1. Our sense of spiritual evil and evil actions (manifest through our conscience) is acknowledged by virtually every religion and culture.

2. As a result of our sense of evil, most people have a need for divine redemption or reconciliation. This is what makes religious reconciliation and the Examen Prayer so important.

With respect to the first point, C. S. Lewis in *The Abolition of Man* presents eight principles that are common to almost every religion and culture.[50] He notes that these eight principles are also

---

[50] Lewis's eight principles: the Law of General Beneficence; the Law of Special Beneficence; Duties to Parents, Elders, Ancestors; Duties to Children and Posterity; the Law of Justice; the Law of Good Faith and Veracity; the Law of Mercy; and the Law of Magnanimity. See C. S. Lewis, *The Abolition of Man* (New York: HarperOne, 2001), appendix.

part of our interior makeup—Christians would say they are part of our conscience. When we violate these principles, we feel or sense it in guilt, shame, and alienation. Volumes have been written about these three negative conditions, showing how powerful this sense of morality and evil is. See for example, Franz Kafka's *The Trial*, Fyodor Dostoevsky's *Crime and Punishment*, and Edgar Allan Poe's "The Tell-Tale Heart."

With respect to the second point, the vast majority of us who are gripped by guilt need some form of spiritual or divine reconciliation or redemption. Without it, we can be reduced to a state of despair like that of the woman I mentioned in the Denver hotel. Our conscience moves us not only to divine reconciliation and redemption but also to the desire to improve our relationship with the Divine—to become more like that reality in truth, justice, and love. The more we imitate the divine essence and goodness, the happier we become—being at home with the Divine, being in harmony with others, being at home with our authentic selves, and being at peace in our conscience. This kind of peace, harmony, and home are sought by almost everyone—of various religions and cultures as well as nonreligious individuals.

In the next chapter we will talk about the Examen Prayer, which is a way of dialoging with God about imitating His goodness and love—not only in the Ten Commandments (which are present in almost every culture) but also in higher forms of love.

Knowing Where We're Going

There's one other point about acknowledging the spiritual world that makes us happy. We know where we're going.

I don't mean that we know exactly what Heaven is like or when we'll get there. But we know this world is temporary. There *is* an eternal world, and we're headed there.

That's why I dwelt on the scientific evidence for life after death. It's not just to show that there is a world beyond the material. One of the consequences of that knowledge is that we have a reasonable degree of certainty.

Uncertainty is one of the leading causes of unhappiness. Look at any of those lists that rank countries by happiness. You'll find that the ones at the bottom of the list are the ones where life is uncertain. They're the ones where you can't tell what's going to happen to you from one day to the next.

We hate uncertainty.

Life is always going to be uncertain here on earth. But if we are open to at least some of the evidence and reflections in the previous chapters and "strive by our deeds to do God's will as it is known to us through the dictates of our conscience, we can attain eternal salvation."[51] This makes the uncertainty a lot easier to take. We hate sitting in the dentist's chair, but we know it's going to be over in half an hour, so we can sit still. We hate the uncertainty of life on earth, but we rationally believe that we have a better life waiting for us, so we can take that uncertainty for just one lifetime.

So let's suppose that you've decided to make that leap of faith. You've decided to join a faith community, and you've been praying. How do you know you're doing the right thing?

This is where faith pays off. You'll discover that you have some inside information about God and His will. We Christians call it inspired revelation.

You're on your way! But changing the things you *do* is only one part of setting yourself up for happiness. You must also change the way you *think*.

---

[51] See Vatican Council II, Dogmatic Constitution on the Church *Lumen Gentium* (November 21, 1964), no. 16.

16

⋘⋙

Transforming Inside

We know that bad things are going to happen to all of us. Sickness and death and plain old bad luck will come. But we also know that some people can go through all those experiences and still be not just contented but happy. Some of the most cheerful people I've ever met have been in a hospice, a place where people are, to put it bluntly, waiting to die. What was their secret?

The element that makes those people cheerful in spite of everything life can throw at them has to be something on the inside, doesn't it? It isn't in their external circumstances. We went through that when we talked about our Level 1 desires: you see people who have everything life could offer them — millions or billions of dollars, houses, yachts, luxury cars, and more health than they know what to do with — who are still miserable. And you see people who have nothing, and that nothing is about to be taken away from them, and they're still cheerful. What's going on?

What those people have accomplished — maybe unconsciously, but it's still an accomplishment — is what you want to work on now. They've made an *interior transformation*. They've changed the way they look at the world, so that their happiness doesn't depend on external circumstances anymore. It depends on themselves and their relationship with the Divine.

The Four Levels of Happiness

As you know by now, I'm a Jesuit. I'm not going to tell you that you should be a Jesuit too (although I'm not going to discourage you if you really have a vocation). But I mention it because I think the Jesuits—and especially their founder, St. Ignatius of Loyola—have some very practical wisdom to offer that will do everyone a lot of good, even if you're not a Jesuit, and for that matter even if you're not a Christian.

One of Ignatius's most important practices is the *Examen Prayer*, a method of praying that directs our attention to exactly what we need.

The Examen Prayer

This is a prayer that will take about ten minutes out of your day. That's not much to ask of yourself. But those will be ten minutes well spent.

The name comes from the Latin word for an examination or consideration. It goes back ultimately to the name of part of a balance, the kind that you would use to weigh goods in the market. And that's what you'll be doing. You'll be looking through your own mind and carefully weighing the things you find there.

But *please* don't think of it as a pop quiz or a final exam. You're not back in junior high school! The whole purpose of the prayer is to bring you closer to God as a person. It's not the kind of examination where you get a grade. No one is going to give you an F. Instead, this should be a part of your day that you look forward to because you're going to spend some time thinking about *good* things rather than your struggles and annoyances.

The way I pray the Examen Prayer, it has two main parts:
1. In the first part, I put myself in a *grateful* state of mind.
2. In the second part, I try to fashion my heart in the mold of the *Beatitudes*.

Gratitude

We can start with that old saying, "Count your blessings." You probably heard that from your parents or teachers when you were complaining about something, and it probably annoyed you. But it's a good place to start anyway, as long as we remember Aristotle's principle of moderation.

Ignatius tells us to put our minds into a state of gratitude. Remember the good things you have and be grateful for them. Remember the challenges you have to face and be grateful for them too.

Now, when I mentioned Aristotle's principle of moderation, I meant that you shouldn't push yourself to be grateful too hard or too early. Let's say you've just received a cancer diagnosis. Do you feel grateful for that? No. Right now, you feel miserable. If you tried to force yourself into telling God how grateful you are for this extra challenge, you'd probably just make yourself sarcastic: "Oh, yes, thank you very much for the cancer, God. How about some kidney stones too? I mean, why stop now?"

Obviously, that's not going to improve your relationship with God. You're going to think God is just being nasty to you for no good reason.

Instead, I'd suggest an attitude of humble resignation. Trust that God knows what He's doing and ask Him to bring something good out of this challenge, even when you can't see how that's possible (you may want to use some of the prayers on the starter list in the previous chapter). Don't try to feign gratitude you don't feel—partly because God will see through it but mostly because *you* will see through it.

You *will* come to be grateful for these challenges later on, if you keep the right frame of mind. I learned to be grateful for the disease that attacked my sight. That doesn't mean I was happy about it at the time. But when I think back now to all the good things that came from it—how it introduced me to people I wouldn't have known, how it made me a better person than I would have been—I can't help feeling grateful. That feeling is *genuine*. It's not me trying to make the best of a bad situation: it's my mature and sincere feeling about what happened to me. But the gratitude didn't come all at once, and I think it would have been destructive if I'd tried to force myself to feel it too early. At best I would have been lying to myself, and at worst I might have become weaker in faith.

So you can start with the things that are easy to be grateful for. You have life. You didn't earn it: it just happened. That's a point to be grateful for. Think of the good friends you've known. Think of the breakfast you had this morning. If you get enough to eat, you're better off than a lot of people on this earth. Think of the mind you have, capable of looking for better things and understanding the world around you in a way that lower animals never can.

For a lot of us, this is easy. We have so many good things just by virtue of living in this world: sunsets, flowers, people. Most of us also have far more material wealth than we need for a comfortable existence, even if we feel as if we're struggling. The fact that you're reading this book means you have an education. All these points are things to be grateful for, and for many of us the gratitude will come quite naturally. But it's still important to concentrate on it and make it explicit—to say, "Thank you, God, for all these gifts that I did nothing to earn"—because putting yourself in a position of *gratitude* brings out the better side of you, the side that's ready to move toward the happiness you're after.

I also know that some people will struggle with gratitude. Especially if you're suffering from depression, you may find it hard to be grateful for the gift of life. You may see the bleak side of everything. I understand. I've never had to deal with real depression myself—that's one of the many undeserved gifts I'm grateful for—but I've known many people who did, and I know that it's not something I can just tell them to snap out of. But you can at least tell your intellect to stop cooperating with your depression. Understand that, in any meaningful analysis, you have a lot to be grateful for, even if you don't feel it right now. And focus on the small things you *do* feel grateful for. I don't know what they are for you, but I know that even people who are profoundly depressed have moments of enjoyment. You want to hold on to those moments and remember them when the depression is taking hold of you.

Ignatius recommends, as part of the Examen Prayer, that you thank God for these blessings because, as Creator, He can providentially orchestrate the seemingly random circumstances of life toward a goal that will optimize goodness, love, and salvation for you and the people you touch. If God, as Jesus taught, is really perfect love (perfect patience, perfect kindness, and so forth, as in 1 Cor. 13)—if His will is always to optimize goodness, love, and salvation for you and through you—then you can be sure that He is orchestrating "conspiracies of providence" to help you to this end. He does it in a way that does not undermine your freedom, but subtly, so that you can freely choose and cooperate with His all-loving will.

This is precisely what happened to Ignatius of Loyola. As a young man, he was a dueler, a ladies' man, and an outstanding soldier, which caused him to be quite vain and certainly not a "man for others." During a particular campaign at Pamplona, Ignatius was leading the defense of a fort with an army that was significantly outnumbered by an attacking French army. During the battle, he was hit by a cannonball that shattered his leg, causing him months of pain and recovery in his brother's home, during which there was no possibility of him resuming his former activities. There was not even a possibility of reading about his former activities. The only available books were about the life of Christ and a book on the lives of some Catholic saints. When Ignatius read them, he was inspired in a way that he and everyone who knew him could not have possibly expected: he wanted to be like Christ—and not his former self. Contrary to any natural cause, his desire to be like Christ was so strong that he changed—quite literally—completely.

Ignatius knew that the cannonball, the recovery in his brother's home, and the availability of only lives of the saints and a life of Christ were not random. Though he was not at all a convinced Christian at this point in his life, he knew he could sense a benevolent conspiracy that offered him a path out of debauchery and bravado (which had its desolations) into a sublime life of goodness, love, and eternity. Though he did not understand why the path of Christ and the saints was the path to spiritual freedom and sublime happiness, he knew it was the Truth. We previously called this kind of conviction "inspiration" influenced by God's Spirit.

At this point, Ignatius was convinced of three central truths: that God was present in his life, that God was blessing and inspiring him, and therefore, that God loved him deeply—indeed, unrestrictedly. He felt there was only one appropriate response: to thank God for the blessings—that is, to express his love for God in return. This sincere expression of thanks and love was for him the path to deepening his relationship with God, which led to increased trust in God's loving providence.

As we express our gratitude to God, there is one point about which we should be careful. It's best not to think about how much you have to be grateful for compared to *that* person, whoever that person is. That brings you right back to the comparison game, and you won't have any trouble finding people who are better off than you: "She has a million, and I only have *half* a million! What do I have to be grateful for?" You may think that's silly, but I can tell you it's a more realistic example than you'd like to believe.

Instead, focus on the things *you individually* have to be grateful for and not on how they compare to the things Jeff Bezos has to be grateful for. There's a lot that's good in your life—absolutely, not just relative to other people.

And I do think you should learn to be grateful for the times of suffering—not too soon, and don't try too hard, but do learn to recognize how even suffering, and perhaps especially suffering, worked providentially for your good. You can think back to bad events or experiences that happened quite a while ago to start with. "If I had never broken my leg," you might say, "I would never have read all those great books that summer. If I hadn't failed algebra in junior high, I wouldn't have had to take the one class that made me really understand how math works." You can probably think of examples like those from your past life, even if more recent events are too hot to touch right now.

The bad things that happened to you in the past have made you who you are today. They've made you a person who realizes that there *is* a way to happiness—a light at the end of the tunnel—if you put effort and inspiration into it. You've already put in enough effort to come this far in this book. These past bad experiences can help you feel more gratitude if you reflect on them for a while and realize how they shaped you. But I caution you again: if they bring up resentments and frustrations more than gratitude, you're probably reflecting on something that's too sensitive for now.

One practice I know a lot of people have found helpful is to write down blessings as they occur to them. At any given time, you may only be able to think of a few things you'd be grateful for. But then a little while passes, and you think of something else.

Write it down. You might keep a blessing journal in the room where you usually pray, and you can gradually watch it fill up with points you're grateful for. One family I know keeps a gratitude jar on the table by the front door, with little slips of paper and a pen beside it. When you think of something you're grateful for, you can write it down and stuff it in the jar, and then when you want to meditate on gratitude, you can pull something at random out of the jar—maybe something you wrote, maybe something somebody else wrote. Either way, it was a good thing that happened to you or somebody you love, and now you have a reminder of it in your hand.

Now, here are some particular things to look for when you're picking out points to be grateful for.

1. Pay special attention to all those messages you get from the Spirit. The more you meditate on them, the more grateful you'll be to God for taking care of you when you needed taking care of, and the more you'll see the patterns in God's providence. As we saw before, those messages can come in the form of opportunities or in the form of suffering, but if they led you to a better understanding of your purpose in life, thank God for them.

2. Look for the good in other people and be grateful for that. Be grateful for it even if it didn't directly benefit you, just because it made the world you live in a better and happier place. Did you see someone in a parking lot help a poor stranger get his ancient pickup truck started again? Was there someone at work who volunteered to take on an unpleasant duty just because it seemed like the right thing to do? These are things you can be grateful for.

3. Be grateful for the good things that happen to *other* people around you. Aside from the fact that the good things are good in themselves, your natural human empathy will make *you* happier because *they* are happier. Your life is better because good things happen to other people.

Though being grateful interiorly is a great gift, being grateful to God—the Creator who guides, inspires, and loves you personally (even through suffering)—is an even greater gift, because it helps us recognize God's love and guidance, which helps us deepen our relationship with Him in prayer and life. As Ignatius might say, the more we express wonder and love at God's blessings, the more we see Him in the events in our lives. And the more we see Him, the more we interact with Him in our daily pursuits. We become like Tevye, the protagonist in *Fiddler on the Roof*—who is constantly dialoging with God on his milk route. "On the one hand ... But on the other hand ... But then again ..."

And now on to part 2 of the Examen Prayer, where we try to conform our hearts to the heart of God through the Beatitudes.

The Beatitudes

Beatitudes is a fancier word for the "Blesseds," because this is a list of blessings pronounced by Jesus. They seem like paradoxes, but if we want to understand what real Level 4 happiness looks like, they're the best place to look.

It helps to put this speech in context. In Matthew's Gospel, near the beginning of His public ministry, Jesus goes up to the top of a hill with a big crowd gathered around Him and preaches a long sermon expressing the heart of His message to all of us.

Christians remember it as the Sermon on the Mount. In it He gives us a summary of His thought, and it all begins with this list of beatitudes. Some translations begin each one with "Blessed are," and other translations begin each one with "Happy are," but they amount to the same thing. Jesus is about to tell us that the people we consider unfortunate are really the fortunate ones.

There are eight of these sayings in Matthew 5 (and a similar group in Luke 6). Two of them are simple promises, though even those imply some disposition of the heart and mind in us, His hearers. The rest are specific directions for forming our attitudes on how to live.

Blessed are the poor in spirit, for theirs is the kingdom of heaven.

Blessed are those who mourn, for they shall be comforted.

Blessed are the meek, for they shall inherit the earth.

Blessed are those who hunger and thirst for righteousness, for they shall be satisfied.

Blessed are the merciful, for they shall obtain mercy.

Blessed are the pure in heart, for they shall see God.

Blessed are the peacemakers, for they shall be called sons of God.

Blessed are those who are persecuted for righteousness' sake, for theirs is the kingdom of heaven.

Blessed are you when men revile you and persecute you and utter all kinds of evil against you falsely on my account. Rejoice and be glad, for your reward is great in heaven, for so men persecuted the prophets who were before you. (Matt. 5:3–12)

There are good reasons for including the Beatitudes in our prayer, but they all boil down to this: the Beatitudes are nothing less than Jesus' definition of love and His plan for a happy life. This is why they sound so paradoxical: because Jesus has to shock us out of our complacent assumptions. That's what we've been doing throughout this book, but now that we've come this far, we can examine these sayings in detail. I think you'll find that Jesus is showing us the way to claw our way up out of the mire of Level 1 and Level 2 into the lasting contentment of Level 3 and Level 4. He's giving us His definition of love so that when He says, "Love one another," we'll know what that looks like. (For an interesting comparison, go back to Paul's definition of love in 1 Corinthians 13 and see how, in spite of using completely different words, it corresponds exactly with this one.)

What Jesus wants for us, and what we want for ourselves, is to be happy like God. This is why we're going to spend this time conforming our hearts to Jesus' standards.

Blessed are the poor in spirit

The poor in spirit are the humble-hearted. What does it mean to be humble-hearted? We hear so little of humility as a virtue in our culture that we hardly know what to make of it. We talk a lot more about pride, which the medieval theologians put at the top of the list of the seven deadly sins—and for good reason. But humility? Isn't that a character flaw?

What humility or being "poor in spirit" means is not thinking you're better than most people. This was a struggle for me when I was young, and it's one of the reasons I've learned to be grateful for my eye problems. I think that was what was needed to cure my arrogance, or at least put me on the road to a cure. In order to do the things I was good at, I had to accept help from other people to do the things I was becoming really bad at—ordinary activities like writing, driving, reading, and so on. I might know more about astronomy than most people, but most people get around better than I do.

The Four Levels of Happiness

I hope you don't need a big physical disability to teach you that lesson. It's much better if you can start learning it now. The more you learn to feel that humility, the happier you'll be.

Being poor in spirit means you can love everybody regardless of their social or economic status. It's surprising how easy it is to fall into the trap of accepting or rejecting people on superficial grounds like that. We may not even know we're doing it, because so much of our social interaction is automatic. But the more we learn to realize that we're no better than other people, the more people we are capable of loving. I probably don't have to point this out, but it's also true that other people tend not to like you as much if they can tell that you think you're better than they are.

We should also remember that the blessedness/happiness of humility applies *right here* and *right now*, not just in the future in Heaven. Humility is a quality that will make you happier the more you apply it to your own life. Stated in our terms, humble-hearted people are saved from the significant anxieties of the comparison game, damaged relationships, and the emptiness of a life without purpose beyond ourselves. Furthermore, humble-hearted people deepen their love of others and God. So there's a good reason Jesus starts with this one. It's the basis of everything else He's going to tell us.

Blessed are those who mourn
Those who mourn (are sorrowing) shall be comforted. This is one of the promises; it doesn't give us a specific dimension of love to work on, but it still tells us something about how we should deal internally with the things that happen to us. When Jesus says that you'll be comforted, He doesn't just mean that you'll eventually get over it, whatever it is.

I remember having a discussion with someone who couldn't see what Jesus was driving at here. "That's like saying it's great to hit yourself on the head with a hammer, because it feels so good when you stop," he said.

"Well, that's not really what Jesus means," I tried to explain. And I don't know how well I explained it to him, but you have the advantage that you've already read most of my best arguments. Suffering of all kinds is unpleasant — that's why we call it suffering. But we can be sure that God will bring something good out of even our worst suffering, if we have faith and patience. It's hard, of course: no one is going to tell you it's not. And I'll remind you of what I said about trying too hard to be grateful too early: don't do it. When you're mourning (sorrowing), just offer God a prayer of trust and leave it in His hands. The blessings will follow. This has certainly been the case in my life — including blindness.

Blessed are the meek
Meek is another one of those words, like *humble*, that we don't really know what to do with in our culture. We think someone who's "meek" is a pushover, someone who will never get ahead in life because other people keep cutting in line. Meek people are too shy to get what they want. They let other people walk all over them. You hear about "assertiveness training," but when was the last time your company wanted to send you to meekness training?

This is a mistaken view of meekness, at least as Jesus meant it — having a *gentle* heart. Jesus meant we should be like Him. He was as gentle and as kind as He could be, even to people who didn't return the kindness. But He was not a pushover. He was sure of His convictions and firm in what He believed, and when something important was at stake, He didn't shrink — not even if it meant He had to die on a cross. But He was focused on the best in people; He tolerated them in their weakness, forgave them as often as they asked, and encouraged them. This is the meekness we should imitate. And when Jesus says that the meek shall inherit the earth, you notice that He doesn't put it off till we get to Heaven. This, once again, is advice for right now, and it will improve our happiness in this world, not just assure us of a place in the next eventually. How so?

The path to gentle-heartedness begins, as we have seen, by looking for the good news in the other. Those who look for the good news in others form long-term empathetic bonds not only with spouses and children but even with friends and colleagues at work. People who look for the bad news and are intolerant, impatient, and unforgiving have not only weak marriages (without emotional intimacy) but also very few friends, and those friendships are based not on emotional bonds, care, and commitment but on esteemable characteristics (such as being a winner, respected, wealthy, and popular)—short-lived if you don't stay ahead of the Joneses.

Blessed are those who hunger and thirst for righteousness
What does it mean to hunger and thirst for righteousness? Is Jesus expecting a high standard I'll never meet?

Take a good look at this saying again. You'll notice that Jesus doesn't say, "Blessed are the righteous." In fact, if Jesus had trouble getting along with any group of people, it was those who thought they were righteous. Jesus would end up being killed by people who thought they were righteous.

So what this saying is talking about has to be something else. Hungering and thirsting for righteousness means you don't have it yet. You *know* you're not perfect. But you also know that God's way is the best way. This is what brings you blessings: wanting to conform your will to God's will. As we've already seen over and over, that is the ultimate route to happiness.

So if you think you're righteous already, you probably have to go back to the first page of this book and start over. But if you've learned to understand that God's will is best—even if you haven't managed to conform your will completely to His yet—then you're on the right track, and you're headed for happiness if you keep on that track. Now you have to learn how to cooperate with God's plan and not work against it, which is exactly what we've been doing in this book.

Blessed are the merciful
We sometimes think of mercy as a virtue for people in power. A judge can be merciful in his sentencing. A conquering general can be merciful to the conquered. God can be merciful to sinners. But how can I, an ordinary human, be in a position to be merciful?

For Jesus, being merciful implies two things: forgiveness and compassion.

As soon as we mention forgiveness, we realize that we do have a kind of power over other people. We have the power to forgive or not to forgive. And this is a more "powerful" power than most of us realize because it implies the power to perpetuate a cycle of misery or end it right now.

We humans have a strong sense of justice, especially when it means justice to ourselves. I think I've mentioned before that one of the first arguments a child learns to make is "It isn't *fair!*"

When someone does something that harms us, whether it physically hurts us or just damages our property or makes us feel angry, our first instinct is usually to find a way to give that person *what he deserves*. We determine what he deserves. But, of course, the person who did whatever it was to us doesn't think he deserves that. If we make him suffer what we think is some equivalent pain, then he'll be just as angry as we were, and he'll want to make sure we get what we deserve.

The Four Levels of Happiness

History is full of family feuds that continued through genera-
tions, an endless cycle of revenge that no one would break because
"honor" demanded revenge for every injury.

But forgiveness cuts right through that cycle of resentment and
violence. When you forgive, the circle is broken.

It may be hard to forgive someone who has really offended your
sense of fairness, especially if it seems that the person did it out
of deliberate mean-spiritedness. That does happen. Sometimes
people can do things just to be mean — although even being mean
usually has another motivation behind it, like proving that I am
more powerful than you, or keeping myself from losing the respect
of the people I think are important. It can also happen because
the person craved the adrenaline rush of a good fight. Anger can
become an addiction.

I know that, especially in our culture today, a lot of people think
of forgiveness as weakness. It's not. Forgiveness is ultimate power.
If you refuse to forgive, you continue that cycle of resentment and
violence, and what happens then depends on who's momentarily
stronger. But if you do forgive, you end the cycle right now, and
there's nothing anybody can do about it. That's why I say forgiveness is ultimate power: it puts you in complete control.

But, of course, it's also giving up power. If you have it in your
power to injure somebody, that makes you feel very important — for
a while. It won't last, though for a while it feels good to feel important. But we're looking for lasting happiness, and forgiveness lasts.

If it offends your sense of fairness to forgive someone, you can
also take the time to remember that you need forgiveness too. You
may be saying to yourself right now, "Yes, but I've never done anything as bad as what *she* did." That's not a good road to go down.
Someone will always be standing in the road further on to point
at you and remind you of something *you* did that was pretty bad.

So what can you do if someone has done something that you have a hard time forgiving?

I understand. I've had to deal with a lot of different kinds of people, and most of them have been delightful. But, every once in a while, I find someone who takes a personal dislike to me, and I've known people who tried very hard to make life miserable for me personally. When that happened, I can tell you, forgiveness wasn't my first instinct. My first instinct was to *get back at them.*

But that's the wrong instinct. What I'd recommend is what I eventually did: trust God to take care of it. If there is an injustice that needs correcting, God is powerful enough to correct it. Offer a little prayer of trust: "God, in this situation, I trust You to do what's right both for me and for this other person, and I'm going to leave it in Your hands." This should satisfy your sense of justice because you know you can trust God to be just.

If you need an example of what perfect forgiveness is like, take a look at the example Jesus gives of His heavenly Father in the parable of the prodigal son (in chapter 16). Though the father represents God, our Father, the parable gives us an example of the ideal of forgiveness that *we* are meant to aspire to.

But there's also a character in the story who represents our natural human instincts. The father has another son who stayed with him faithfully the whole time, helping him run the household. "It isn't *fair!*" says this brother. "You never gave *me* a big party! I've done the right thing this whole time, and what do I get for it? Then this no-good ingrate brother comes back, and you give him *everything!*"

You recognize these feelings at once because all of us have them. But the father in the story points out that his faithful son has had all the comforts and luxuries of home, and it's a very rich home, all this time—and besides, he will inherit absolutely everything from his father. He shouldn't be thinking about what's fair. He should be happy that his brother has wised up and come back to the family.

Like all Jesus' parables, this one compresses a lot of insight into a short space. But the main point for us right now is that we have to be forgiving, even when our human instinct is telling us that it's not *fair*. When we do forgive, we make room for the possibility of a renewed relationship with the offender, and we give the offender a chance to redeem himself and start over. This brings both Level 3 and Level 4 happiness.

Compassion is the other component of the mercy Jesus wants to see in us. Remember the story of the good Samaritan (Luke 10:30-37). A man was beaten and robbed and left for dead on the road. Along comes a priest, and he sees the mess and goes to the other side of the road. It might be a dead body, after all, and if the priest touched a dead body, he would be ritually unclean and have to go through a long process to get purified again—and who wants all that trouble? So he passes by and pretends not to see. Then comes a Levite (another member of the priestly class), who responds the same way.

Priests and Levites were the images of *worthy* people for the Jewish scribe whom Jesus was talking to. But now, in the story, a Samaritan comes down the road. Samaritans were members of a caste that orthodox Jews despised. They were heretics; they practiced the religion in the *wrong way*, and—as the New Testament tells us elsewhere—Jews avoided them. But the Samaritan stops, takes care of the beaten man (who may in ordinary life have despised him), then brings him to an inn and pays for his lodging and all incidental expenses.

That's the kind of compassion Jesus wants from us, and He showed His Jewish audience this quality in a Samaritan to shock them out of their assumptions of what was right and proper. Who was the good guy in this story? The one that Jesus' audience believed was despicable. "Go and do likewise," says Jesus.

Here we see again how all the Beatitudes are interconnected. You need one to understand the rest. You won't be *merciful* unless you're also *poor in spirit*. Jesus knew the scribe He was talking to thought he was better than other people—and *especially* better than the Samaritans. "Well," said Jesus, "I have a story about that ..."

So what are we supposed to do? Are we supposed to prowl the roads looking for people who have been beaten and robbed? Well, you can do that if you think you'd be good at it. (I don't think I would be.) But we all have different talents and therefore different ways we can help someone in need. Frequently enough, we don't have to look for the marginalized; they come to us.

Once in church we had just begun the Mass when someone who had obviously been drinking wandered in from the street. His clothes were filthy. He smelled awful. He had obviously slept in the street the night before. He sat in a pew toward the back. Immediately one of the impeccably dressed ladies nearby moved right next to him, and for the rest of the Mass she showed him where we were in the missal so he could follow the liturgy with the rest of us—which he did. It was a small action, perhaps, but it was something she knew how to do. And maybe it was the first evidence that man had seen of love in action in a long time.

Blessed are the pure in heart

What does it mean to be "pure in heart? Basically, to be sincere. I know I have insincerity in my own heart. I build facades, and sometimes I'm not even true to myself. Unsettled grudges still nestle in there. I have periods when I'm cranky and have to work not to show it.

And that's normal. But it *is* important to work on cleaning up the insincerity and hardness because—as Jesus tells us all through the Beatitudes—our interior disposition is what makes us happy or miserable.

If you read the Gospels, you find that the recurring villains are the self-righteous Pharisees. Now, it's important to point out that the Pharisees had a lot of virtues. They learned Scripture thoroughly, and they were serious about following the rules.

But being serious about following the rules was their problem. They had hundreds of ceremonial rules to follow, and they thought that virtue was a matter of following the rules. Though this is partially true, and rules do have a part to play in forming the direction of our moral compass, rules can always be twisted to our advantage. Jesus watched self-righteous Pharisees twist the rules to mean that they didn't have to take care of their own aging parents, or that they didn't have to worry about the poor if the poor weren't up to their standards of virtue. So Jesus taught His followers to respect the rules but to follow them with compassionate and sincere hearts. When we lack a compassionate and sincere heart, rules by themselves can lead us away from the humility that's so hard to maintain—and right down the road to thinking we're better than everybody else. We become like the Pharisee in the story: "God, I thank thee that I am not like other men."

Blessed are the peacemakers

Peace is a complex idea for Jesus and for the people who were listening to Him when He preached from that hilltop. It means more than just "not fighting." It also means being aligned with the will of God.

So a peacemaker is not just someone who reconciles enemies, although that is definitely one of the things a peacemaker does.

It's also someone who helps others find their way to peace with God. You can do that by introducing them to the Gospel, but you can also do that simply by taking away the things that keep them from knowing love to its fullest extent. Are you encouraging others around you to find happiness through humble-heartedness, gentle-heartness, and contribution—or are you modeling the culture of comparison and greed? A peacemaker breaks through the comparison game and helps others do the same.

Blessed are you when men revile you and persecute you
and utter all kinds of evil against you falsely on my account
We're blessed when men revile us and persecute us—this is another one of the promises. Obviously, we don't control what other people say or do to us. But notice, once again, what a *meek* person is like. When you're being reviled and persecuted, you don't give in. You stand strong for what you know is right. You also resist the temptation to take revenge and give as good as you got. That, again, is strength. Jesus expects strength in meekness, because if we let the ill winds of insult and persecution push us around, we'll never be able to do any good that others resist. We have to have the courage to follow the path we know is right *and* the courage to forgive those who insult and revile us. As noted before, one of the best ways to do this is to entrust the offender and the situation to God—"Lord, You're the just judge, please take care of this person and situation."

Making the Beatitudes Our Own

So we've gone through all the Beatitudes, and we understand what's expected of us. Now what? How do we make this part of a daily prayer?

Well, remember that Pharisee? "God, I thank thee that I am not like other men." You don't want to be like that.

So let's think about the first beatitude: "Blessed are the poor in spirit." Should you make an all-out effort to be humble?

I don't think you'll succeed if you do. I *do* think you should start acting *as if* you actually felt the humility you're striving for, but I know human nature—my own nature—well enough to know that humility is hard. If you do work really hard at it all by yourself, you're likely to be discouraged by your lack of progress. Or, worse yet, you'll be proud of your success. "Look how humble I am!" you'll think to yourself. "I must be the humblest person on earth!" And then you've become that Pharisee.

Instead, I look at that first beatitude and remember that Jesus really is poor in spirit—humble-hearted. He is humble enough to come to anyone, even me, as a friend. And since He's right here, because I'm praying to Him, I ask Jesus, "Help me learn from You. Help me be poor in spirit along with You."

Then I go down the rest of the Beatitudes, especially the six that give us specific instructions for happiness, and I treat them the same way.

First, I think of how Jesus exemplifies that attitude of heart.

Then, I ask Jesus for help in turning *my* heart in that same direction.

The point is that you don't just *decide* to have the interior virtues Jesus points out to us. You can't just decide and be done with it.

But that's why you do this prayer every day. It works in your mind, slowly getting you used to new habits of thinking. Instead of dwelling on your resentments, you're looking for things to be grateful for. Instead of dwelling on how much other people annoy you, you're looking for the best in them. Instead of trying to be in control of everything, you're admitting that you can't always be in control and you're asking for help from God, who *is* in control. Slowly, as you keep doing it, the prayer does its work—with God's help.

Now let's review the two steps in the examen prayer—gratitude and the Beatitudes:

1. *Gratitude.* Spend five or ten minutes counting your blessings for the day—not necessarily the experiences you enjoyed the most (although it's certainly good to be grateful for those too), but those that brought more faith, hope, and love into your life.

2. *The Beatitudes.* Now consider one or more of the Beatitudes. Normally, I pick just one of them for the day and think about that one. Consider how Jesus lived that one truth and ask for His help to be a little more like that. Think about what your day was like today. Did you exemplify that beatitude? Where could you have improved things in your dealings with the people around you? Ask for help wherever you see problems, and trust that the help will come. Don't try to think too deeply about exactly what you should have done. Identify the problem, and ask for Jesus' help to solve it.

If you do this *today*, you won't be a perfectly happy person tomorrow. But if you do it *every day*, the little things will add up, slowly, into big changes. That's why I tell you to moderate your expectations. Don't try to fix everything that's wrong in your life. Just use this prayer to make slow adjustments to your way of thinking.

Did you ever have braces on your teeth? An orthodontist looks at your mouth and says, "This tooth should be over *here*, and this one should be back *there*," and so on. But no orthodontist thinks that can be done *right now*. Instead, your orthodontist makes minute adjustments, a bit at a time, each going in the right direction, but each tweak so small that you can't tell the difference from one day to the next.

The Four Levels of Happiness

You can think of the Examen Prayer as something like braces for your heart, except that it's a whole lot less expensive. But it's doing the same thing. By making small adjustments day by day, you rearrange your ways of thinking and feeling until your heart is working as it's supposed to work—your priorities are lining up more and more with God's. You'll never be completely perfect in this world (any orthodontist who promises you a *perfect* mouth is exaggerating), but you'll move closer and closer to lasting happiness.

Once you've been doing this prayer for a while, you can learn more about the way St. Ignatius did it. His version is a little more complicated, although not a whole lot. I've given you a good place to start, but all you have to do is look up "Examen Prayer" online, and you'll find good information. Start with this simple version, and when you've been doing it for a while, you'll be ready to step up to the more advanced level.

17

≪≪≪

The Rest of Your Life

I know you're not perfectly happy right now. You won't be perfectly happy tomorrow either. Or the day after that.

But I do think you may be a little happier already than when you started on this journey. And I do think your contentment will increase over time, and you'll get closer and closer to the happiness you desire—if you keep on the path.

So let's review.

You started out on this journey because you realized you weren't really happy. Most people today are in the same boat. And happiness is the ultimate goal of human existence.

Happiness is the fulfillment of our desires. But what we learned is that there are four levels of desire, and so four levels of happiness:

1. Material needs and basic instincts
2. Comparison to others
3. Empathy and service
4. The transcendent

We climb those four levels like a ladder, and if we stop anywhere along the way, we don't reach our destination. All four levels are necessary to our happiness.

In order to reach the destination, then, we're going to have to make a leap of faith and, if we can't affirm the transcendent, at least *assume* it. I think I've shown you why that faith is *reasonable*. But it does take faith, and you have to act as if you believe in the world of the spirit even when you don't feel fully convinced. If you do, odds are that you will become progressively more attuned to a spiritual reality inspiring, guiding, and even loving you.

Once you've made that leap of faith, the two essential components are a faith community and a regular practice of prayer. I also recommend the Examen Prayer of St. Ignatius of Loyola, which I think is so useful that it will help you even if you aren't a Christian.

Are people who follow this path really happy? We've seen that people who are focused almost solely on Level 1 (pleasure) and Level 2 (ego-comparative) are dogged by the negative emotions of the comparison game—inferiority, superiority, fear of failure, fear of loss of esteem, jealousy, contempt, loneliness, emptiness, and much more. Though on one level they seem happy, the majority are deeply conflicted, depressed, and angry—and they make the people around them feel the same way. It's not surprising, then, that Level 3 (contributive) and Level 4 (transcendent/spiritual) people tend to be much happier in life, even if they have more than their fair share of suffering.

Furthermore, people who are religiously affiliated tend to be significantly happier than those who are not.[52] We might expect

---

[52] There are many studies showing the relationship between religious affiliation and happiness, as well as the relationship between nonreligious affiliation and significantly increased depression, anxiety, substance abuse, familial tensions, suicide attempts, and suicides. Among them are the following: Kanita Dervic et al., "Religious Affiliation and Suicide Attempt," *The American Journal of Psychiatry* 161, no. 12 (December 2004): 2303-2308, https://doi.org/10.1176/appi.ajp.161.12.2303; Harold Koenig, "Religion, Spirituality, and Health: A Review and Update," *Advances in Mind-Body Medicine* 29, no. 3 (2015), https://pubmed.

this if God exists and made us in His image. This is consistent with the transcendental desires we discussed (in chapters 8 and 11) and the scientific evidence we discussed about the rationality of the universe and life after death (in chapter 12).

As we saw, it's not enough to simply *believe* in God or an afterlife. We must enter into a *relationship* with Him because our happiness consists in being in relationship with Him and trying to become more like Him. Virtually all religions believe that God is loving, and Jesus emphasized this in His teaching that God is like the father of the prodigal son—the compassionate, gentle, and supportive father who forgives his son for all the outrages he has committed against his family, country, law, and God Himself. Jesus addresses Him as "Abba"—the gentle, affectionate, compassionate, trustworthy "Dad" or "Daddy."

The Beatitudes—those simple statements Jesus made at the beginning of the Sermon on the Mount (Matt. 5)—are Jesus' definition of love and the pathway to happiness. So the path to happiness includes being humble-hearted (poor in spirit), gentle-hearted (meek), hungry for righteousness, forgiving and compassionate

ncbi.nlm.nih.gov/26026153/; Raphael Bonelli et al., "Religious and Spiritual Factors in Depression: Review and Integration of the Research," *Depression and Research Treatment* (2012), https://doi.org/10.1155/2012/962860; Stefano Lassi and Daniele Mugnaini, "Role of Religion and Spirituality on Mental Health and Resilience: There Is Enough Evidence," *International Journal of Emergency Mental Health and Human Resilience* 17, no. 3 (2015), https://www.omicsonline.org/open-access/role-of-religion-and-spirituality-on-mental-health-and-resilience-there-is-enough-evidence-1522-4821-1000273.pdf; Edward Alan Miller et al., "The Protective Effects of Religiosity on Depression: A 2-Year Prospective Study," *The Gerontologist* 56, no. 3 (June 2016): 421–431, https://doi.org/10.1093/geront/gnu073.

(merciful), pure of heart, and a peacemaker. It so happens that multiple studies validate this—humble people are happier and more effective leaders than the proud; forgiving and compassionate people are happier and more effective leaders than the unforgiving and hard-hearted; the authentic are happier than the inauthentic; and so forth. Beyond all this, if God really is love as Jesus insists, then He, too, is humble, gentle, forgiving, compassionate, pure of heart, and a peacemaker, which strongly implies that His promise of eternal happiness will be quite real if we try to become like Him. If so, this is a path to true happiness worth investing in.

That's where we've been. As for where we're going—well, it looks a lot like where we've been, but much better. We continue on the right track for the rest of our lives. We keep up our connection with the transcendent. We keep up our practice of prayer. Slowly, day by day, week by week, year by year, we learn *how* to be happy. After a lot of practice, we get to be really good at it.

To get to that point, however, we have to make the decision. You can't skip the work needed to get to the end of the journey. There's no royal road to happiness. But it starts with the one thing you can do now. *Decide* to be happy. It really is your decision. No one else can *make* you happy—or miserable.

Decide to be happy. And then do the work that makes happiness possible.

About the Author

Rev. Robert J. Spitzer, S.J., Ph.D., is the founder and president of the Magis Center. A scholar, teacher, author, and seasoned leader, Spitzer is a preeminent theologian and philosopher, specializing in the philosophy of science. His other areas of expertise are ethics and leadership. As president of Gonzaga University from 1998 to 2009, he significantly increased the university's programs in faith, ethics, service, and leadership as well as the enrollment, endowment, and facilities. Spitzer has made many TV appearances, including *Larry King Live* (discussing the origins of the universe with Stephen Hawking and Deepak Chopra), *The Today Show*, the History Channel's *God and the Universe*, and the PBS series *Closer to the Truth*. He has a weekly television program on EWTN—*Father Spitzer's Universe*—and is the author of eighteen books and many scholarly articles.

Sophia Institute

Sophia Institute is a nonprofit institution that seeks to nurture the spiritual, moral, and cultural life of souls and to spread the gospel of Christ in conformity with the authentic teachings of the Roman Catholic Church.

Sophia Institute Press fulfills this mission by offering translations, reprints, and new publications that afford readers a rich source of the enduring wisdom of mankind.

Sophia Institute also operates the popular online resource CatholicExchange.com. *Catholic Exchange* provides world news from a Catholic perspective as well as daily devotionals and articles that will help readers to grow in holiness and live a life consistent with the teachings of the Church.

In 2013, Sophia Institute launched Sophia Institute for Teachers to renew and rebuild Catholic culture through service to Catholic education. With the goal of nurturing the spiritual, moral, and cultural life of souls, and an abiding respect for the role and work of teachers, we strive to provide materials and programs that are at once enlightening to the mind and ennobling to the heart; faithful and complete, as well as useful and practical.

Sophia Institute gratefully recognizes the Solidarity Association for preserving and encouraging the growth of our apostolate over the course of many years. Without their generous and timely support, this book would not be in your hands.

www.SophiaInstitute.com
www.CatholicExchange.com
www.SophiaInstituteforTeachers.org

Sophia Institute Press is a registered trademark of Sophia Institute.
Sophia Institute is a tax-exempt institution as defined by the
Internal Revenue Code, Section 501(c)(3). Tax ID 22-2548708.